JAMES HOBAN

Designer and Builder of the White House

JAMES HOBAN

Designer and Builder of the White House

STEWART D. McLAURIN
with
Matthew R. Costello
Merlo Kelly
Kristen Hunter Mason
Andrew McCarthy
Christopher Moran
Brian O'Connell
Finola O'Kane
William Seale

THE WHITE HOUSE *HISTORICAL ASSOCIATION*

THE WHITE HOUSE HISTORICAL ASSOCIATION

The White House Historical Association is a nonprofit educational Association founded in 1961 for the purpose of enhancing the understanding, appreciation, and enjoyment of the Executive Mansion. All proceeds from the sale of the Association's books and products are used to fund the acquisition of historic furnishings and art work for the permanent White House collection, assist in the preservation of public rooms, and further its educational mission.

BOARD OF DIRECTORS

John F. W. Rogers, Chairman
Teresa Carlson, Vice Chairperson
Gregory W. Wendt, Treasurer
Deneen C. Howell, Secretary
Stewart D. McLaurin, President

Eula Adams, John T. Behrendt, Michael Beschloss, Gahl Hodges Burt, Merlynn Carson, Jean Case, Ashley Dabbiere, Wayne A. I. Frederick, Tham Kannalikham, Metta Krach, Martha Joynt Kumar, Anita McBride, Barbara A. Perry, Frederick J. Ryan, Jr., Ben C. Sutton Jr., Tina Tchen

NATIONAL PARK SERVICE LIAISON

Charles F. Sams III

EX OFFICIO

Lonnie G. Bunch III, Kaywin Feldman, David S. Ferriero, Carla Hayden, Katherine Malone-France

DIRECTORS EMERITI

John H. Dalton, Nancy M. Folger, Janet A. Howard, Knight Kiplinger, Elise K. Kirk, James I. McDaniel, Robert M. McGee, Ann Stock, Harry G. Robinson III, Gail Berry West

EDITORIAL AND PRODUCTION STAFF

Marcia Mallet Anderson, Chief Publishing Officer
Lauren McGwin, Editorial and Production Director
Kristen Hunter Mason, Senior Editorial and Production Manager
Elyse Werling, Editorial and Production Manager
Rebecca Durgin Kerr, Editorial Coordinator
Ann Hofstra Grogg, Consulting Editor

DESIGNER

Pentagram

COPYRIGHT © 2021 WHITE HOUSE HISTORICAL ASSOCIATION.
All rights reserved under international copyright conventions.
No part of this book may be reproduced or utilized in any form or by any means, electronic or mechanical, including photocopying, recording, or by any information storage and retrieval system, without permission in writing from the publisher. Unless otherwise noted, all photographs are copyrighted by the White House Historical Association.
Requests for reprint permissions should be addressed to:
Photo Archivist, White House Historical Association,
PO Box 27624, Washington, D.C. 20038.

FIRST EDITION
10 9 8 7 6 5 4 3 2
LIBRARY OF CONGRESS CONTROL NUMBER: 2020950332
ISBN 978-1-931917-96-4
PRINTED IN ITALY

To William Seale (1939–2019)

and

*To those of many nations, both free and enslaved,
whose labor built the President's House.*

Contents

INTRODUCTION		STEWART D. McLAURIN Meeting James Hoban	1
NARRATIVE	I	WILLIAM SEALE James Hoban: Designer and Builder of the White House	4
	II	MERLO KELLY The Building Line in Ireland	29
	III	FINOLA O'KANE Eighteenth-Century Irish Landscape Design and Its Translation to America by James Hoban	35
	IV	CHRISTOPHER MORAN Life as Lived in Irish Country Houses: Desart Court and Leinster House	40
	V	BRIAN O'CONNELL James Hoban and George Washington Devise the President's House	46
	VI	ANDREW McCARTHY James Hoban's 1792 Designs for the President's House	56
	VII	MATTHEW R. COSTELLO Building the President's House with Enslaved Labor: James Hoban and Slavery	72
	VIII	KRISTEN HUNTER MASON James Hoban and the Early Roman Catholic Church in the Federal City of Washington	76
CATALOG	I	Irish Influences	86
	II	The Builder in America	150
	III	Remembering James Hoban	190

ILLUSTRATION CREDITS—192   ABOUT THE AUTHOR AND CONTRIBUTORS—196
ACKNOWLEDGMENTS—199

INTRODUCTION

Meeting James Hoban

THE FAMOUS MEETING THAT ULTIMATELY GAVE America its White House occurred in 1791 in Charleston, South Carolina, when George Washington happened to be introduced to a young "practical builder" from Ireland. Washington was impressed by the builder but soon forgot his name. When considering the design of the President's House, yet to be built in the emerging Federal City of Washington, the president asked after the young builder. Soon James Hoban appeared in Washington's Philadelphia office with his credentials. By 1792, Hoban was at work on the building site, having won the competition for the design of the President's House. Washington had placed him in charge of the entire project, with all carpentry, stonemasonry, and brickwork under his supervision. The resulting structure, accomplished in time for President John Adams to take residence in November 1800, fulfilled Washington's vision and is today one of the most recognizable landmarks in the world. Yet of the millions of people who know the White House, most, like President Washington, are likely to find Hoban's work more memorable than his name.

James Hoban the man is, in fact, somewhat elusive, with only one portrait known to have been made during his life, and with that being a silhouette, we only see half his face. His birthplace in Ireland was demolished as were his home on F Street in the City of Washington and one of the greatest influences on his work, Desart Court, the grand Irish country house he knew in his youth. His first design concept for the exterior of the President's House has been lost, and his papers burned in a house fire after his death. Nevertheless, when the surviving traces of his life and times are assembled, a fuller picture of his life and work emerges. With this anthology, the world's most knowledgeable scholars on James Hoban introduce us to him, presenting the story of his life, influences, and work. Church records in Ireland and Washington, D.C., preserve the dates of his baptism and marriage. A stone monument marks the site of his grave. The monumental buildings known to Hoban that still stand in Dublin and in the Irish countryside provide a tangible connection to Hoban's concept for the President's House. Hoban's surviving letters to the Commissioners for the District of Columbia further enrich the history. Newspaper advertisements and census records remind us that the President's House was built with enslaved labor and that Hoban himself owned slaves.

More than two hundred years after Washington and Hoban met in Charleston, I have met James Hoban myself, through my role as president of the White House Historical Association. I have admired the carvings in stone he oversaw above the North Door, studied the historic walls of the mansion from every vantage point, and stood in the rooms within the house he envisioned. My travels to Ireland further deepened my knowledge of Hoban and his work. Standing in one of the oval rooms of what was the Newcomen Bank, I was reminded of the oval rooms designed by Hoban for the President's House. And surveying the exterior of Leinster House, I was inspired by the very architecture that inspired Hoban.

As the White House Historical Association celebrates its sixtieth anniversary, it is fitting that we celebrate the work of the elusive designer and builder who created the White House. Together the Irish, British, and American scholarly perspectives presented in this volume provide a proper introduction to the man whose life's work is known so well.

Stewart D. McLaurin
President, White House Historical Association

Stewart D. McLaurin is seen in one of the oval rooms in what was once the Newcomen Bank, in Dublin, Ireland (previous spread, 2018). James Hoban's design for the distinctive oval rooms on the south side of the White House reflect the influence of the oval rooms at Newcomen Bank, which Hoban would have known during his training in Dublin. The oval shape is seen in the Blue Room on the State Floor of the White House (opposite, 2019).

I. WILLIAM SEALE

James Hoban: Designer and Builder of the White House

James Hoban is remembered as the designer and builder of the White House. Take that from him and he sinks into obscurity as a local builder during the founding years of Washington, D.C., who was there from the city's inception to his death in the last month of the year 1831. Information about the man is scattered, even in his limited environs, and he exists mainly in public records for his work on government projects. His personal records—such as letters and documents—were destroyed, it seems, when his house burned after his death.

Had any of Hoban's papers and more of his drawings survived, fire or not, it probably would have been an accident of fate. Families move and disburse possessions; in the haste of time, old trunks filled with papers can be uninteresting unless their contents have some magic of history or financial value attached to them. But even that magic can be forgotten or become of less interest as time passes, and all the more so when the surviving papers represent a mere house builder, be he the builder of the White House or not.

Most of the written documentation of the Irish-born Hoban that exists relates not to the man but to his work on the White House—notes, reports, contracts.[1] In addition to this are three significant touchstones preserved from his personal life: a miniature wax portrait of himself, perhaps made while he was in his 40s; a prize medal for architectural drawing from the Dublin Society; and his medal for designing the White House. Instead of the medals, he could have had substantial cash prizes, but he chose the medals, which he treasured.

As for drawings, there are few, and it is clear that most of those Hoban made or approved are missing. We know secondhand that he had White House drawings framed under glass hanging on his wall, but only because Charles Bulfinch's tracings of these, made in 1829, are filed in the National Archives and were used in building the North Portico. It is assumed that the originals were returned to Hoban's house and were lost in the fire. All that we have of Hoban are a few things he owned and references to more than thirty years of work on the White House.

This chapter brings together what we do know about Hoban, of his life and work in America and the building of the White House. It takes otherwise a contextual approach, painting pictures that describe the world he passed through. The great Irish estate where he grew up and the city of Dublin, Ireland, where he was exposed firsthand to fine construction and design under tutelage from the leading Irish architect Thomas Ivory, are described in other chapters in this book. What is important for the story in this chapter is to know that Hoban's hands had been dirtied at a young age in the workingman's art of building, and his experience appears to have been comprehensive, from carpentry to stonemasonry. Where his prime expertise lay cannot be certain. But he was knowledgeable enough to direct and stand by it all.

THE IRISHMAN SETTLES IN AMERICA

James Hoban's first documented appearance in America is in a notice he placed in the Charleston and Philadelphia newspapers in May 1785, which broadcast his skill:

> *Any Gentleman who wishes to build in an elegant*
> *Style, may hear of a person properly calculated for*
> *That purpose who can execute Joinery and Carpenter's*
> *Business in the modern taste apply James Hoban.*[2]

It is prophetic that he advertises himself as a builder of fine houses. He may have spent time in Philadelphia, and it is likely for the simple reason that an Irishman held America's Philadelphia in very high esteem as the home of liberty and a place of unlimited opportunity. Since Philadelphia was the center of culture and the most prosperous city in the newly independent nation under the Articles of Confederation, naturally it would appeal to a young Irish immigrant. And in Dublin, where he had received his experience in building, Philadelphia was considered almost a sister city, admired for the sort of spunk and ambition attributed also to Dublin.

Whatever Hoban's first port of call, if Philadelphia, he, like many others in his era, lacking personal connections, may have found the building trades very crowded. Even Thomas Jefferson had to labor to find a stonemason willing to leave Philadelphia and work in Washington. In any case Hoban soon found himself in Charleston, South Carolina, on the doorstep of Pierce Purcell, an established local carpenter and probably one of his cousins originally from Ireland.[3]

At this time in the late 1780s Hoban was in his early 30s, and he may have looked like his wax portrait, the only image we have of him. It shows a very Irish-looking, healthy young man, with ruddy complexion and thick, reddish hair brushed forward in the fashionable Titus mode of the time, crowning in Roman style a long, oval face. To further interpret the wax miniature: his expression might be called inquisitive, but no less eager for what is to come in the vast and changing world into which he has cast himself. The medal he brought with him from Ireland boasts his successful schooling in architectural drawing and suggested to those who saw it a valuable knowledge of building engineering and a practical experience in working on large buildings. He could point out what he had achieved under the supervision of Thomas Ivory in Dublin and doubtless carried with him letters of recommendation. The silver medal engraved to him was for "Drawings of Brackets, Stairs, Roofs, &c," presented to him by the Dublin Society. Its School of Architectural Drawing, which he attended, was a public institution available to further the education of promising young men. Hoban had been wise in accepting the medal instead of its alternative, a sizable prize of cash, an appealing reward in itself. Money spent was money gone, however, and the medal would be of value to him all his life. And it was.[4]

Soon enough Hoban was in partnership with Purcell and lived with the Purcells at 43 Trott Street (later Wentworth Street) in the Ansonborough addition to the old city, in a house Purcell built doubtless with future speculation in mind, a house later demolished and replaced with probably a better house. Hoban built a house next door, which he occupied or rented out until he sold it in 1798, when he no longer planned to live in Charleston.[5] Unknown to him when he built this house, his intention to build country houses would be more than amply fulfilled.

In the partnership of Hoban & Purcell, Pierce Purcell was very aware of the value of his new, young partner's qualifications in attracting business. Hoban had Irish credentials in a city with prominent Irish politicians and national statesmen, and others of note besides. The tone of Irish society was high and the will to build grandly certainly current. Hoban and Purcell were tradesmen, neither ones members of the Irish Roman Catholic Hibernian Society. But they made themselves visible in other ways, as founders of St. Mary's Catholic Church, the first in Charleston, and, curiously, also founding members of the Masonic Lodge of Charleston.[6] And some buildings of their era in Charleston, long attributed to amateur "gentleman architects" such as the venerable attributions of several buildings to Judge William Drayton Sr., may well have been theirs.[7]

While we do not know for certain what the partnership built except for Purcell's house and Hoban's, their notable and best-documented triumph was in gaining the contract for building the Charleston Theater, and there is mention of planning funding for an orphans' "asylum." Postrevolutionary wealth of the Low Country plantations and the new flowering of the port created a major consumer class in Charleston that longed for the luxury and culture associated with cities such as Philadelphia, New York, and London. A fine theater was one of the main ornaments to a city, and Charlestonians began a subscription to pay for one projected by its ambitious design to be as grand as any that could be found.

Descriptions of the proposed theater published at the time attribute the building to Hoban, and it was probably designed by Hoban, with guidance from actors and theater managers from Richmond, Virginia. It gives us a glimpse into his design capabilities. It was to be a very large building on Savage's Green, covering most of a triangular lot fenced with iron palings. The theater itself was to seat more than a thousand patrons in addition to handsome box seats supported by columns and lighted with patent luster lamps of glass. Carpentry was required in paneling, railings, and a wooden inner structure painted specifically in polished French white, while the exterior was stucco over brick, scored to resemble ashlar. Everything modern taste could call showy elegance was to be seen in profusion at the Charleston Theater. The reality would be simpler by the time it was built, but Hoban by then had gone away to build the President's House.[8]

As the partnership developed, Purcell clearly became Hoban's promoter, himself taking otherwise a secondary role. The arrangement developed slowly but it endured; the two were comfortable with it. Circumstances strongly suggest that they rebuilt the burned-out Charleston State House, which placed them on the edge of the then current controversy over retaining Charleston as capital of the state. Public records of the rebuilding were destroyed in the city fire during the Civil War, and most of the information about the rebuilding is circumstantial. Yet a thread runs through the subject that makes it very likely that Hoban may have been prominently involved, and his references later on were influenced by that building.

Charleston, the capital of South Carolina, had long used a State House built in colonial times. As the traditional center of politics, it boasted its power and prestige. But the presence of a new Constitution in 1789 rather freed up the state's sense of historical obligation and dependency upon Charleston.

Moreover, the old State House had burned to its walls in 1788, taking away the practical argument in the city's favor of already having a capital building. The legislature decided to move to Camden, inland halfway to the mountains, and then changed its destination to Columbia, a new town more favorable to the heart of the state by river and wagon road than Camden. In a rush to alter history's course, the adherents of Charleston as state capital hurriedly rebuilt the old State House.

The reconstruction went quickly. The look of the finished State House was fresh and in a style not at all unfamiliar in the Anglo-Irish architecture both Hoban and Purcell had known in Ireland. Moreover, it was a simple architecture, an ordinary rectangle with a forward centerpiece of four attached Ionic columns mounted atop an arcaded projection from the basement level. The mode was common enough in Europe for public buildings, as town halls, but it was the first of its kind in America.

Was the State House remodeled after the fire by Hoban & Purcell? There is not a single other supportable claimant. Yet the only evidence that seems to connect the building to Hoban & Purcell is that the main advocates of the State House rebuilding were Irish Americans, avid supporters of preserving the seaport of Charleston as capital of the state. But attributing the building to a single architect or builder must remain a question. The site of the state capital settled at Columbia, and the rebuilt State House became the Charleston County Courthouse.

PRESIDENT GEORGE WASHINGTON'S CHALLENGE

Meanwhile, the new Constitution authorized Congress to create a Federal District as the nation's permanent seat of government. In 1790 Congress passed the very controversial Residence Act, which established the capital at a totally new location, in a new city to be built on the Potomac River some 160 nautical miles by sailing ship from the Atlantic Ocean. It was hoped that, with improvement, the Potomac would connect the coastal regions with the West. The states of Virginia and Maryland would contribute to the 10 square mile site. Although Thomas Jefferson, as secretary of state, supervised planning for the relocation of the government, George Washington himself assumed responsibility for the design and building of the city, and he appointed the immigrant French engineer, Pierre Charles L'Enfant, to make a city plan. The president was committed to the Potomac River location. His wishes silenced most opposition.

In late spring 1791, when President Washington made the southern branch of his nationwide tour, his new city was very much on his mind. To L'Enfant's preliminary suggestion to build a splendid modern city, like the capitals of Europe, he mused over the two buildings specified in the Residence Act—a house for the Congress and a house for the president. An advertisement was prepared and published, inviting investors and builders to the new site. Washington had determined to fix the city to the ground as best he could and as soon as he could, so he selected the President's House as the first priority—the smaller building—and the Capitol Building second.

The president's rule on his tours was not to stay as a guest in private homes, so the Charlestonians rented a fine three-story mansion to house him and his entourage (today the Heyward-Washington House Museum). Having such a private place, he could have intimate meetings within its protective walls and schedule public appearances when he went outside, saving his strength otherwise, for his schedule was exhausting.[9] During this official visit to Charleston, James Hoban was presented to the president by General William Moultrie, Jacob Read, Henry Laurens, and other prominent residents, as a man of genius in building, his credentials apparently extolled. This must have taken place in the Heyward-Washington House, for public exposure of the president attracted crowds in too great and noisy numbers for interviews up close. Washington remembered not Hoban's name but the event of meeting him, and the prominent Charlestonians, many Irish, who introduced him. Perhaps some conversation ensued about the Federal City.[10]

Pierce Purcell must have been along as well, or at least knew the possible importance of the introduction. Some months after the Charleston encounter, he traveled alone to the Potomac to inspect the site where the city would be built. For the day-to-day work, commissioners had been appointed by Washington, paid by reimbursement, no salaries. The commissioners were responsible for every improvement in the Federal City, including plans and sale of lots, all subject to Washington's approval. Through Read, Purcell managed to gain an appointment with Commissioner Daniel Carroll at the site of the Federal District. Carroll was the holder of most of the land necessary for the new city. L'Enfant's plan had been revealed in 1792 to the general astonishment of government officials, who looked warily toward the short deadline of the first Monday in December 1800 for occupancy of the new capital. Purcell saw only farmland, pastures, orchards, some low brick cottages, and ruined buildings. L'Enfant's avenues, fountains, monumental buildings, and public parks were only on paper. But thanks to pressure from the president, the site was not entirely silent. L'Enfant had negotiated to buy a downriver stone quarry at Aquia Creek and to lease others. He had a team of laborers on a ridge digging on cellars of what he called the "presidential palace." And the surveyors had begun laying out L'Enfant's plan on the ground, making such practical alterations as the terrain suggested.[11] After Purcell returned home, Read and Carroll corresponded about Purcell's visit to the Potomac. Carroll was amused to say that Purcell had spoken more of the absent Hoban and his sterling credentials than of his own abilities.[12]

President George Washington, 60 years old in 1792, showed deep concern over getting the city-building started. He met frequently with L'Enfant, politicked behind the scenes with Republicans and Federalists, agreeing to lend support to many policies he might otherwise have opposed or questioned, just to assure that the city would be on the Potomac River. Since his youth he had believed the river, with the removal of natural rapids, could form a belt of economic communication and prosperity that would perpetuate Virginia's once flourishing Tidewater and agricultural lands thereabout. Mount Vernon, downriver from the city, was, of course, part of this idea.

But what of the new city? That it rise free of the machinations of existing political power bases in Philadelphia and New York was essential as part of the scheme and a fresh concept to bind together the nation of states. For if the project were to fail, the government would be returned to New York or remain in the present capital, Philadelphia. At this point the president, besieged with everyone's ideas, conflicts, and complaints, had the notion of employing a practical builder for the first house, that of the president: a man of skill who was a builder, not a dreamer. He recalled that in Charleston his friends had presented to him just such a man, a man of proven skill, and substantial education. It went without saying that the man must communicate easily with the president.[13]

Washington himself took command and asked after the "practical builder" to whom he had been introduced in Charleston. He could not remember James Hoban's name but had been favorably impressed at the time. Soon Hoban assembled his references, including the premier one from the patriot Henry Laurens, and placed these in the president's hands in Philadelphia, having appeared without invitation.[14]

Hoban had illustrations of houses that might work. We can only guess what some of these were, although it is highly possible that he owned Robert Pool and John Cash, *Views of the Most Remarkable Public Buildings, Monuments and Other Edifices in the City of Dublin*, published in 1780, its authors students in the drawing school Hoban attended. Included were some of Thomas Ivory's buildings where Hoban had worked. Meanwhile a wary Jefferson had pressed the commissioners building the city to launch a competition for house designs, so concerned was he with what the president might decide upon left to his own resources. Already he and L'Enfant had spread before Washington pictures of chateaus and big houses for inspiration. Jefferson seems to have feared another house on the model of Mount Vernon, while Washington had seen the odd Roman temple Jefferson was building for the Virginia State Capitol. On March 14, 1792, the commissioners announced a competition "for a president's house to be erected in this city."[15]

The competition entries were, according to the president, even worse than what he had seen from Jefferson and L'Enfant, with colonnades and courtyards; one had a throne room.[16] Competition drawings or not, Washington wanted a house, not a monument, and told Hoban to proceed on his own. Obviously what Hoban presented was more desirable to the president than the drawings of the other competitors. Jefferson entered secretly and was rejected. Leading builders, such as New England's much-celebrated cabinetmaker Samuel McIntyre, made their bids, but none pleased Washington, who stuck unyieldingly to Hoban.

If ever there was a rigged competition it was this one. Hoban went to the Federal City—which had been named "Washington"—and gave the commissioners a letter of recommendation from the president, a general sort of letter: "I have given him this letter of introduction in order that he might have an opportunity of communicating his views & wishes to you, or of obtaining any information necessary for completing the plans. But as I have no knowledge of the man or his talents further than the information which I recd from the Gentlemen in Carolina you must consider this letter merely as a line of introduction for the purposes mentioned."[17]

The commissioners met at Suter's Tavern in Georgetown, the principal hostelry in the area, owned and managed by a Scot named John Suter. It was from this tavern that most of the action emanated in the early years of the Federal City. L'Enfant had stayed and worked there, with his models and drawings for the city. L'Enfant's plan was approved there, under serious pressure from the president, and at Suter's the competition for the President's House was judged.

SOURCE OF THE WINNING DESIGN

It is well documented that the White House in its essentials is designed after the mansion in Dublin that was the principal residence of the Duke of Leinster, the leading and most widely respected peer in Ireland. This house, a country house in town built in the 1740s, was the basic model for the White House, with alterations. The winning design was first drawn out on paper by James Hoban and then redrawn by Hoban with alterations dictated by Washington, reaching final form in the fall of 1793. Why was Leinster House selected as the model? There was the appropriateness of a "house for a gentleman" of course, and this appealed to Washington. But might there have been a more timely reason in the dramatic appearance at the same time of the duke's legendary younger brother, Ireland's beloved Lord Edward?

Hoban was surrounded by political issues that can only have interested him. First was the new Constitution of the United States. Then there was also his likely involvement, perhaps by way of the State House reconstruction, in the efforts of Charleston to remain the capital of South Carolina. The capital's designation was a hot, statewide contest. Yet even more presented itself across the Atlantic.

A rising protest back home captivated the Irish in America, including the vibrant group of Irish in Charleston. This was the ups and downs of political anger between the Ireland, the home they all remembered, and the immovable British overlord that was its master. The now famous organization, the Society of United Irishmen, began in Northern Ireland as a public celebration of the principles of French Revolution of 1789 and the promise of the liberation of Ireland by forces from revolutionary France. The British made a harsh and bloody response, which touched off violence. The United Irishmen became increasingly radical, resorting to guerrilla warfare in their plea for an equitable constitution like the one produced in the United States. The emotional bitterness of the Irish more than matched the bloodshed against them, still chilling and unfair when read today in the yellowed reports of the time.

The efforts of the United Irishmen to achieve an independent Ireland captured the sympathy of many Charleston Irish, who believed the Irish protest of the 1790s comparable to the American Revolution, in which violence was also kindled by Britain's refusal to compromise on the colonists' demands. Very many Irish Americans, remembering an oppressed Ireland firsthand, had come to America to escape it. This one can assume was at least a reason Hoban, like so many others, emigrated. In his case he appears to have left a busy career in building, in part serving his master Thomas Ivory. Maybe he simply wanted more.

Most Irish sympathy in America, and not least that in Charleston, was drawn especially to the rebellion's popular and symbolic leader, Edward FitzGerald, the young Anglo-Irish aristocrat who dazzled both sides in the American Revolution with his dramatic skills on the battlefield. Lord Edward, as he was known, was the younger brother of William FitzGerald, the second Duke of Leinster, and had fought as a British soldier in the Revolution. Seriously wounded in 1781 in the Battle of Eutaw Springs, he had spent a long recuperation in Charleston, where he mixed freely with the community. Lord Edward was a celebrity wherever he was, but he was blessed as well with a particular witty charm and love of life that drew people to him on a human level. He was an aristocrat enriched with a common touch.

Lord Edward left Charleston at war's end and, living for a time in Paris, became a convert to ideas of Liberty and Equality that nominally had led the French Revolution of 1789. He was at the heart of the events, sharing the liberal philosophy with "The Égalité," the Duc d'Orléans, and living quarters with the great essayist and publicist Thomas Paine. Longing to be a hero and always praising his native Ireland, Lord Edward became from Paris the leading popular supporter of the United Irishmen and an ardent advocate of the proposed invasion of Ireland by the French. At first Lord Edward's performance seemed to Irish Americans a childish rebellion against his own class, but when, to his great disappointment, the French lost all interest in carrying out the promised invasion, Lord Edward's heroism was then praised in Ireland. With support he became more brazen and returned from France in secret to become commander in chief of the United Irishmen in a protest now styled a revolution against the British.

Charlestonians still remembered the charming enemy during his convalescence in their city, guest in the house of a relative of George Washington. His lordship was young, dreamy, handsome, and flamboyant. A decade later, imbued with popular principles of Liberty, Lord Edward, living in a Europe smoking with the fire of revolution, had committed himself to becoming the symbol of an independent Ireland. He publicly denounced his own aristocratic title as an Irish peer (although he would never be able to shed the name "Lord Edward"). Upon his secret return to Ireland, and his involvement in terrorist activities, the British authorities tried with little luck find his whereabouts. Leinster House was ransacked in a search for him. He evaded his British predators and participated in raids himself, boldly, until his luck ran out.[18]

Is the White House, designed in the rising time of Lord Edward's patriotic fame and modeled on his family's official Dublin residence, a forgotten reminder of him and not, as one might otherwise presume, of his stately brother, the "First Gentleman" of Ireland? Any number of houses could have provided a model.

In the competition for the design of the President's House, Hoban had the leading hand. He drew his competition entry on paper under the watchful eyes of the commissioners and showed his work to the president when he was in town. It is probable that only Washington saw drawings of what the house would look like—the main facade and perhaps the plan of the main floor, which he had already modified or "Americanized" from the complex model of Leinster House. But the facets of the facade must remain in question, because Washington was yet to make his final alterations. Whatever was on the table that summer of 1792, Hoban seems easily to have won the prize and, as was his custom, took for it a medal instead of the alternate cash purse of $500. We know what we do about the competition because some of the entries ended up in Jefferson's possession as secretary of state and this included Hoban's winning entry, which was the one that combined a facade with a modified plan.

Both of Hoban's entries were evaluated by Washington; of that there can be no question. The first was similar to Desart Court, the stately country house in County Kilkenny that Hoban had known as a tenant's son growing up. The dominant exterior feature was a pedimented colonnade raised over a high ground-floor basement, the columns reaching over the second and third floors. This was ultimately rejected. On the one drawing of this first competition entry a floor plan is delineated; but this plan fits the revised competition entry, which is worthy of note as similar to Leinster House in Dublin.

The first competition entry for the President's House is unknown in detail, but it is known that Washington modified it to his satisfaction in a 1793 autumn meeting with Hoban and the commissioners, increasing the volume of the house by 20 percent and reducing the height from three to two stories over a ground-level basement. In that drawing, which survives, the Leinster House image is very clear, with pediment and window hoods, attached Ionic columns, smooth ashlar walls, and broad pediment over the central, columned section. Washington also increased the proposed stone carving on the exterior, while admitting that such elaborate carving had become less popular than it once had been. The resulting house, yet on paper, became the President's House, which we know as the White House.[19]

RIVAL BUILDERS BEGIN THE PRESIDENT'S HOUSE

President Washington continued as patron of the 1793 plan. He gave his total trust to Hoban, over that to the commissioners. Such a volunteer commission as he had appointed proved difficult to manage. For example, under the president's direction Hoban was put in charge of building the house. All "departments" were under him—carpentry, stonemasonry, brickwork. That is, he was to receive and recommend bids for construction work in all its details on behalf of the commissioners. The commissioners knew nothing about building. Worried about money, they were sometimes at odds with Hoban's recommendations.

In one instance the commissioners went around Hoban and Washington himself in hiring. John Suter was privy to nearly all the commissioners' meetings directly or otherwise. He tended to meddle. He heard the commissioners complain about the monumental task of building the house of stone—Washington required that the public buildings be of stone to support what L'Enfant had convinced him was needed for them to be permanent, as in the great structures of European capitals—and that stonemasons were difficult to lure to Washington because they were so busy with work in Philadelphia and New York. Suter had a suggestion: a cousin of his, one Collen Williamson, a stonemason from Scotland who had immigrated to New York bearing excellent references. Without delay Williamson appeared at the tavern, mingling with the commissioners and educating them on his qualifications.

A man well into his 60s, Williamson was boastful of his Scottish experiences, making special note of his years of work in the Highlands for the powerful Grant family, leading landholders of Scotland, as well as his carrying out of designs made by the celebrated Adam brothers, Scottish architects with practices in both London and Edinburgh. But when the commissioners rather capriciously welcomed Williamson as their superintendent, they obviously created a problem. Washington had selected Hoban as the man in charge, and the commissioners, impressed with Williamson, had given the management job to him. Hoban was a general builder, Williamson primarily a stonemason. At the time it seemed that if everyone behaved himself, it would all work well, an easy beginning typical in building that promised room for all.[20]

Williamson hired both slaves and freedmen to prepare the site. L'Enfant had already dug huge cellars to accommodate his big plan. Because a smaller house was being built—smaller than L'Enfant envisioned but larger than Hoban's original plan—these foundations had to be partially filled, requiring temporary retaining walls. The house was to straddle a high ridge that extended to Georgetown going west and to the site of the new Capitol Building going east. The location of the President's House foundations was shifted a bit by Washington himself. When Williamson faced the commissioners with how to fit the smaller foundations into the larger one—whether to favor the north, south, east, or west—the commissioners hesitated, lest their decision displease the president. An impatient George Washington, himself a trained surveyor, went personally to the site and on August 2, 1792, drove a stake in the ground to locate the North Door of the President's House. Thus the house was centered on its north dimension and the other three dimensions naturally faced precisely on the points of the compass.[21]

Williamson and his stonemasons built the basement or ground floor of the President's House. It was heavy construction, meant to support brick-backed stone walls two stories above it. Internally the soft brick lining behind the outer stone made the basement walls nearly 4 feet thick. On the outside the stone basement walls were formed in bold rustication. To make the burden of the walls above appear all the more powerful, many stones were laid to resemble few. The windows were framed in large, dressed quoin stones and keystones, and all was rendered smooth or tooled, dramatic in massive configuration. It is a masterwork in early American building.

Hoban apparently had little to do with the basement except for nominal management in shipping stone upriver from the quarry at Aquia Creek. He gave his attention at this stage to gathering materials for work yet to come and land on Tiber Creek (formerly Goose Creek). This in itself was a large and complicated task, for transportation on the Potomac River meant avoiding the swift current that ran in the opposite direction. Access to the high ridge of the building site was by a temporary canal rising in four stages from Tiber Creek by locks. Then materials were towed overland by either ox-driven wagons or wooden flats. Over the winter the stone, which was still moist with "quarry sap" or groundwater, had to be packed in straw to protect it from freezing. Lime and brick had to be similarly protected, and two brick kilns were built on what is now Lafayette Park. The logistics of constructing the President's House were much like those used in building monumental buildings a thousand years before. Human innovation had naturally intervened, but in smaller ways than modern man might imagine. The project took place on the knife edge of the Industrial Age. Not until the house was rebuilt by Hoban twenty-five years later would the babel of machine noise accompany construction.

Williamson's work was commended, yet his contract was terminated in the autumn of 1795. The reason for his dismissal had nothing to do with the quality of his work, which was high, but with his manners and his status in the project. He had understood that he was in charge. He resented Hoban's presence, Hoban's youth, and Hoban's skill, and he complained about the building crew that Hoban employed, all Irish, and "vagaboons" to boot, as Williamson described them in his memorandums. He was very clear in his dislike of Irishmen, and Hoban was very clear in his preference for them, but kept his mouth shut most carefully. Williamson made trouble for the commissioners and the commissioners naturally wanted their work to appear smooth-sailing to their august leader in Philadelphia or when he dropped in on trips south to Mount Vernon, which were sporadic but always brought a change of one kind or another. Williamson's dismissal seems to have had more to do with Washington's faith and admiration of Hoban than anything else. Hoban was his man on the job; Williamson was the commissioners' man, and it was no secret where the power lay. Williamson was naturally offended but continued building houses in the area for the rest of his life, occasionally writing an angry letter to the commissioners. Hoban might have but did not leave Williamson high and dry, and his kind treatment of the self-avowed enemy gives a glimpse of the Irishman's character. In spite of hard feelings in the past, Hoban hired him from time to time to serve lucrative roles in evaluating the work of others—the crucial process known as "measurement," before payment was approved. Hoban seems to have felt that the commissioners had not acted fairly with Williamson.

Replacements for Williamson arrived from Scotland.[22] They operated as a lodge of stonemasons, worked hard in their two stone yards, and gave Hoban very little trouble in pushing the work forward. The Scots soon had the walls of the house to within 6 feet of the cornice finished on the ground. They were slowed thereafter only by the process of forming clay models for the pilasters and lush foliation that was to refine, with delicate ornament, the windows and doors.

BUILDING IN HASTE

To a builder's eyes the house at the close of work in 1793 was far along toward completion. To amateur eyes, as those of the commissioners, the work seemed to proceed very slowly. They fussed and worried, harassing workmen at every level, including Hoban. As superintendent of construction, Hoban held power over all aspects of the work. The meddling of the volunteer commissioners, who wished most of all to please President Washington, could be interpreted as grasps of power over him. This was a frail technicality requiring courtesy and a little scheming on Hoban's part, for when the commissioners determined to intervene in some matter, the result was predictably bad. This intervention often took place in the wake of a visit from the president, when the commissioners, excited by the meeting, sought to tighten the ropes of the operation.

Hoban employed his former partner Pierce Purcell as superintendent of all carpentry and woodwork. This assignment involved the processing of quite a large supply of pine and oak (measured by foot and yard), milled under Purcell's direction and at great effort. Most of this material came from sawmills near Elizabeth Town (today Elizabeth City), North Carolina, and the Virginia forests of Stratford Hall, for which Hoban negotiated with the celebrated war hero Henry ("Light Horse Harry") Lee, whose debts at the time concerned the president.[23]

The joined framing of the house within the shell of stone and brick was Purcell's responsibility, and he had collected within a bit more than a year a large store of framing ready to assemble. Abruptly at the end of the building season in December 1794, the commissioners became concerned over costs, reduced Purcell's duties, and demanded from Hoban an inventory of materials in hand. An angered James Hoban, who had received no warning, wrote to them. It is the only letter in this critical tone Hoban is believed ever to have written, and it reveals his natural tact:

> *I am just informed by Mr. Purcell who hitherto has acted under me as Foreman of the Carpenters and Joiners department for the President's House—that one of your humble board has given him Positive orders not to proceed further by any other directions than those which came immediately from the Commissioners, and that henceforward he should have his Instructions from the Board. You will please to recollect gentleman, that, I have furnished the original drawings of that House, that I have entered into a Contract to see those drawings carried into effect, and to this end have hitherto conducted the Building, and consequently held my character as Architect, and Practical Builder responsible for the completion thereof—Thus circumstanced I feel it my duty as superintendent of that Building, to call on your Humble Board for an explanation of this hasty and inconsiderate interference—The carpentry and joiners work of that Building are its Principal Security—now, if you have assumed the direction thereof, Remember you are responsible for the whole.*[24]

This response marked the culmination of complaints that Hoban did not make, because such letters were not his style. He was too prudent to burn bridges behind him. Yet one might easily imagine a certain comfort he felt in his position. There is no way he could not have acknowledged privately the damaging inefficiency of the commissioners, and he surely knew through observation, if not direct comments, that President Washington knew it, too. And on this project, Hoban was Washington's man, playing a role essential to the creation of the capital and its stability, an achievement Washington knew was important to his administration. The number of times Washington and Hoban met is unknown, but it is certain that Hoban kept his mentor informed, whether they met at the site, in Philadelphia, or in Washington's study at Mount Vernon.[25]

Now Washington intervened. He dismissed the volunteer commission and established a new, salaried one. The new commission knew building and the politics of public building. Notable among its members was Dr. William Thornton, an educated physician and an amateur architect of learned skill. His design for the new Capitol had won that competition, and work on that building was also under way. All the new commissioners took to heart the president's desire to complete the President's House. The character of Hoban's authority over the President's House project was never questioned again.

CITIZEN OF WASHINGTON, D.C.

The builder's fortunes also rose. A group of wealthy citizens headed by one Samuel Blodgett of Boston, New York, and London decided to invest in a hotel, there being very few accommodations in the new city. The new hotel was styled the "Great Hotel," possibly because its design was very similar to Hoban's first competition drawing for the President's House; the design also, for what little we know of it, was strikingly like the Charleston State House. Hoban built the Great Hotel, but the investors eventually sold it to the government for offices.[26]

Hoban became known as a house builder and general contractor. No project seemed too small. When Father Anthony Caffry established the first Roman Catholic Church, St. Patrick's, in the Federal District, he turned to fellow Irishman Hoban to build it, which Hoban did. He was convinced that his Irish workmen needed a church and reached into his own pocket for part of the funding. The small red-brick church was eventually replaced, but Hoban's name always was associated with building it. He worked on John Tayloe's Octagon House, an innovative structure fit to the corner upon which it still stands. Designed by his colleague Dr. William Thornton, it was the first private house of note built in the Federal City.

Hoban became one of the first residents of Washington, marrying and living the remainder of his life there. His bride, Susana Sewall, was from an old Maryland Catholic family and may have been a relative of Purcell, for he and the Sewalls were close. After their marriage the Hobans participated in all the aspects of life in the rising capital city. Sources suggest that they eventually had a farm in Maryland, but they were still always in residence in Washington. Hoban placed advertisements for his work in the local press, but he was usually booked up on government projects. He transferred his membership in the Masonic Order from Charleston and became a founder of Federal Lodge No. 1. Here again his being an active and very visible Mason seems to have caused him no conflict as a communicant in the Catholic Church.

The best efforts cannot pin down how many buildings Hoban built or even repaired in the Federal City. One is inclined to think that there were many, if only because of the wealth he accumulated. A building he commissioned on what is now Lafayette Square bears mention if only for the contrast of its architecture to its use. This was called Carpenters' Hall, a generic name common to most big building sites where the carpenters did final shaping of wooden members and where workmen assembled with the superintendent to determine all manner of solutions.[27] This wooden building, which stood approximately where the 1853 equestrian statue of Andrew Jackson stands today, had simple board sides, dimensions about 50 by 25 feet. Here Washington as a residential city was, in a sense, born, for within its walls the Catholics, Presbyterians, Methodists, and Baptists founded their local congregations, and of course the Masonic Order, very important to the builders, made its permanent appearance.

Of his many endeavors, the President's House was still paramount in Hoban's self-image and would be so for the rest of his life. He employed without interference scores of Irish building men and hired slaves from labor agents who supplied them, usually under strict conditions, from their masters. He was disciplinarian over the workmen, be they laborers or skilled tradesmen. The Scottish stonemasons were no trouble for him, but his Irish workmen were. To tighten his control over them, Hoban organized a militia company and required most of them to join, attend drills, and pay dues. While he appears to have been easygoing, he was also a stickler for honest and acceptable work. If a workman was late or absent, a fine was taken out of his wages. James Hoban became "Captain Hoban," a title by which he would be known universally, captain of Washington's first militia, mustered for years from Carpenters' Hall. Looking out for his workers' welfare, Captain Hoban also founded the Sons of Erin, a local society that assisted newly arrived Irish immigrants with housing, provisions, and medical care.

EXTERIOR AND INTERIOR FINISHES

Hoban and Purcell oversaw the heavy, joined timber structure built within the stone walls of the President's House, but the brick inner walls and basement groin vaulting required specialists to be brought in, such as the brick contractor Jeremiah Kale. Kale developed several brick kilns in the immediate vicinity. Most of what he produced in them were soft building bricks never meant to be exposed to the weather, so his kilns were not notably hot. Almost all the bricks were laid in tandem as inner walls, never exposed to the weather; this was not true of the executive offices next door, where the brickwork was external and the bricks on the outside had to be hot-fired.

Weather was a main consideration for the President's House, which was exposed to full, drying sun on the south or "garden front" but subjected to lingering natural moisture on the north or main front. This moisture was compensated for by a deep areaway that kept the building from collecting groundwater and remaining damp from rain. Even today workmen at the White House tell of getting wet from rain on the north, while on the south side, at the same time, sunshine keeps them dry.

Always identified as "architect" of the house, Hoban had charge of finishes, too. He detailed on paper the doorways and windows and any special features the house was to offer. In this capacity he provided drawings for the stonemasons working on the exterior, some of his details coming directly from architectural pattern books current in his time, such as the Scot James Gibbs's 1728 *Book of Architecture*, a perennial classic known arguably to all ambitious builders in Hoban's time. The fine external carvings we see today survived the fire of 1814, when British troops burned the house during the War of 1812. The Double Scottish Rose was as yet unknown elsewhere as a stone-carving motif, but, introduced by the Scots carvers with Hoban's approval, it survives pleasantly and uniquely as a personal touch to the design.

Of the President's House interior—all destroyed in the fire—we know almost nothing aside from a few details suggested by clues in invoices. Written documents suggest that the main floor's doors were surmounted with ornamental entablatures. They specify for certain that the doors themselves were of mahogany inlaid with sweet bay magnolia wood and holly, but the design we do not know.[28] The window sashes were of enormous scale and delicately rendered in mahogany, with interior or sash shutters to complement them. Silver-plated hinges and locks were affixed, whatever design detail these followed being lost.[29] Passages on this main floor were to have been paved in marble, including the large Entrance Hall, but this feature was dropped in favor of wood because of cost of transporting marble. Significantly the brick groin and arched vaulting in the basement were built before this decision was made, and they, if in duplicate since the Truman renovation completed in 1952, remain to be enjoyed today.[30] The columns in the Entrance Hall were built of King of Prussia blue marble from a quarry near Philadelphia. The main stairs were redesigned from what Hoban wanted, to rise in a single range, then divide at a broad landing into a pair of stairs that reached the second floor. President Jefferson built them otherwise.

Simple fireplace mantels of wood formed the bases for applied ornament in cast "composition" purchased from George Andrews of Baltimore. Andrews provided his molded composition ornaments to many houses in the region, his material being refined finish plaster of paris mixed with mortar. The rest of the walling in the house was ordinary plaster on lath and wooden wainscot. Since Hoban designed the interior of the house rebuilt after the fire, we might think the interior details of the second house would suggest what the first house had been like. Yet this would be a mistake, for the interior seems to have originally followed an earlier Georgian taste, which was likely to be heavier and more ornate, not the light, more modern configuration of the reconstruction yet to come.

The house was finished sufficiently to be considered so on November 1, 1800, one month before required by law. Of course it was not in fact finished in its entirety for some years thereafter and would be burned and rebuilt before it could be called truly finished. In the fall of 1800 the plaster walls were still wet and not prepared for paint or paper; whitewash helped hurry them along toward drying. The cabinetry, which seems to have been noteworthy, was not varnished or painted, and Joseph Middleton, the cabinetmaker, had set completion back with private dealings, building for clients of his own when under contract to Hoban for the government project. He set up his shop in the oval room on the second floor and lowered his clandestine products to the ground by rope. What would be called the East Room was a raw brick shell, its finishing postponed for thirty years. A long porch intended for the main floor on the south was not built, although doors cut in the stone to give access to it can be seen on the South Front still today.

Furniture from the rented house that had served as the president's residence in Philadelphia was sparse indeed, but the builders could be glad that it made the voyage at all, for it was nearly lost with the government papers in a storm at sea. President Washington's red-covered parlor furniture, soaked, was piled up in the basement's oval room Hoban intended as a servants' hall. Above that room on each floor were similar oval rooms, the finest being what we know today as the Blue Room, on the main floor, today called the State Floor. The ovals had almost certainly been included by Hoban in his plan on orders from Washington.

Early in the presidency a custom was developed for the president to hold weekly receptions for invited male guests at his official house in Philadelphia. These were conducted in imitation of the weekly receptions by the king of England, as witnessed firsthand by Americans in the diplomatic service. As the men stood in the formation of a long oval, the president and an announcer walked around the oval making pleasantries. Even before occupying the rented house in Philadelphia, the president had ordered the entire rear wall of the dining room removed and rebuilt in a semicircle to accommodate the weekly receptions.[31]

Hoban wrote a report to the commissioners on his work on the President's House from November 18, 1799, to May 18, 1800, six months before Washington's successor, President John Adams, was to occupy the house. In the basement story he said that a wooden floor was being built over the square pavers first laid, in the interest of having dry floors in the rooms. Only three rooms on this level were floored and plastered, although all the new floor joists were set in the south-facing rooms. All the windows were glazed within wood sashes. On the main floor two-thirds of the rooms were trimmed with jamb linings, soffits, back elbows, and grounds. Only four rooms were plastered. The second or residential story was nearly complete, with its eleven rooms plastered and wooden trim in place. Wrote Hoban in his report: three rooms that were finished had "doors, sashes and shutters hung; sub-base, base and plinth put up. The fire place formed with fire stone, and the chimney-piece, architraves to doors and windows and the sub-base ornamented with composition; the sashes glazed and painted; the stucco ornaments, and the walls and ceilings given smooth final finish and applied stucco ornament," the character of which we do not know. He continued with the "Principal stair-case, 19 by 38 feet; back 14 by 28 feet, and private stair-case, 9 by 14 feet are plastered two coats, and one of stucco finishing. The steps, raisers and hand-rails are got out for the principal staircase and nearby ready to put up. The back stair-case is finished, steps, raisers, balusters, brackets and hand-rails. The private stair-case is stepped and the hand-rail getting ready."[32] There were to be three stairs, of which two were ready, a small, twisting service stair to the basement and a better finished private stair to the second floor. The ornamental grand stair, we have seen, remained unfinished at the west end of the Cross Hall that spanned the width of the house. This stair would be changed in configuration by Jefferson, the third president to occupy the house.

The East Room was entirely unfinished and would be until the time of the seventh president, Andrew Jackson. A stately space, it was intended as an "Audience Chamber" where the president would receive petitions from Congress and from citizens. It was huge, 85 feet long and 22 feet high (instead of the 18 feet common to the rest of the main floor), its ceilings poking well into the second floor, where the floors were raised to accommodate it. The room was unfinished because time had not been sufficient to finish it in appropriate splendor and because its purpose waned through the 1790s. After Jefferson's republican victory in the election of 1800 such ceremony as it implied no longer meant anything.

Perhaps the greatest trouble on completion of the President's House was the roof, a situation not unique to building projects of the late 1790s. Care had been taken to select the finest slate for a "permanent" roof. For reasons unrecorded, the roof did not succeed. The slate was stacked on the ground and replaced by a roof largely of split wood shingles. It was by no means an economic decision but one simply to keep the rain out. The failed slates, preserved, were to appear again in Hoban's life and that of the presidency.

As he was finishing the President's House, Hoban was also building a pair of executive office buildings flanking the house. It had been a hard decision to erect tall office structures in the proposed gardens of the President's House, but George Washington insisted that the president's staff be in close proximity to the president, whose office was in his residence. Congress had vociferously opposed having the offices so far from the Capitol, but the president was resolute and had his way. The two office buildings, one on the east for the Treasury Department and one on the west for the State Department and the military were simple, three-story rectangles built by but not designed by Hoban. The foregoing describes the condition more or less as President Adams found the President's House on November 1, 1800, the day the government took possession of it and its surrounding President's Park. Hoban would continue with small projects finishing the buildings for another two years.

DEVELOPMENTS IN DOMESTIC ARCHITECTURE
AND THE RISE OF THE ARCHITECT

The design and construction of the President's House took place for Hoban in a period of transition. When he started the work, at the very beginning, the word "architect" had meaning in Europe, but by the time he finished it was a word increasingly used in the United States to describe an educated engineer with abilities to design as well as construct. Yet to most Americans an architect was simply a builder of one kind or another. He might produce a simple drawing of a plan and elevations, but with few if any directions or specifications. He might show excellence in many separate aspects of putting a house together, from timber work to stone and brick masonry. His expertise might lie in framing, carried out with as few iron elements as possible and "joined" with members and linking elements entirely of wood. His design might have come from his good memory—nearly always the case with the so-called vernacular or everyday traditions. Yet in the eighteenth century architectural pattern books began to be published to assist the builder in producing stylish houses, designing with the help of mathematics and geometry the classical forms their clients wanted. A full library of these books was available to Hoban in the Dublin Society School of Architectural Drawing, as well as the personal guidance of his respected teacher Thomas Ivory.

Architects, in the sense of the term today, comprehensive as designers and builders, were first in evidence at about the time Hoban completed the President's House. Although Hoban apparently had few enemies or even critics, it is through the "corrections" of his work by the main one, Benjamin Henry Latrobe, that we can place Hoban appropriately somewhere between being a tradesman or a builder, in contrast to Latrobe, who is considered by architectural historians as the first "professional" architect to practice in America. He insisted on the use of that professional title, but the line between the two categories is thin.

Latrobe was both an engineer and a designer of buildings. His work in his native England was noteworthy, if not outstanding, but never rose to the quality of his work in Philadelphia, Washington, Baltimore, and New Orleans. The some nine thousand letters and papers he assembled and kept during his American career provide a workshop of sources of a London-trained architect. In 1803 President Thomas Jefferson hired him with the title "Surveyor of the Public Buildings of the United States." His main responsibility was to complete the Capitol, but Jefferson made good use of him at the President's House. Left to his own purposes, Latrobe would have made the house more fashionable and current. Then, after the end of the War of 1812, when the house was to be rebuilt following the fire, he might have had a better chance. But his difficult personality stood between him and President James Madison. Madison preferred the milder-mannered Hoban.

Yet Latrobe's criticisms of the house as it was being rebuilt sharpen the distinction between the approach of a builder and that of an architect. On March 22, 1817, Latrobe wrote to the public buildings commissioner William Lee remarking on Hoban's President's House plan:

> *I feel no delicacy whatever . . . towards Mr. Hoban. If the plan of the house were his design I should be guilty of great professional impropriety in interfering with his operation. But as it is acknowledged as that of the palace of the Duke of Leinster, which I now have before me, in a book containing the principal edifices of Dublin, he cannot be offended even if he should see these remarks. In the first place, I must mention, that the situation of the kitchen is intolerable, and has been a nuisance to every President's family that has occupied the house. It is dark and damp and can never be otherwise: for even the present bridge [built over the areaway to the north or front door] obscures it, and the Sun never visits it. It perfumes the whole house with the steam and smell of the victuals: The operations of cooking, are seen by the Visitors that approach the front door; and it is impossible to prevent cook and the Scullions from throwing dirty water and Ashes out of the windows into the Area. When the weather becomes warm, the windows are opened and the nuisance is almost intolerable.*[33]

The smells and inconveniences of kitchens, nor the likelihood of their being in use all day long, had not troubled people before the new philosophies of private and convenient living that came with the end of the eighteenth century.

Latrobe pointed out that the portico proposed on the north would block out much of the light the kitchen needs:

> *In spite of every contrivance to throw light into the kitchen, Candles must be burned all day long. Now every housekeeper knows that light is a very important requisite in a kitchen in which even not much cooking is going on. A dark kitchen is the first objection made by a Lady to a house which she proposes to hire. But when such dinners are to be dressed as [an event of the] President U.S. light is absolutely indispensable. Darkness is synonymous with filth with dirty dishes, with underdone and overdone and burnt pastry, and with broken china, and casseroles covered with verdigris. Oh the clatter of knives and skewers, and dishes that has assailed me out of the den of a kitchen on going to dine with the President. Had it not been for the savory exhalations that accompanied the rattling of the Irons, you might have supposed yourself listening to the tortures of the dungeons of the inquisition.*

> *In modern usage the kitchen should be beneath the dining room, if there is no way of having it outside in another building, with access to coal, wood, and ice. It is an altogether abominable thing that all the [domestic] offices are below or that they are not vaulted. But that cannot now be helped. But if the family apartments must be in the second story, the evil is increased. From the Housekeeper's room in the Office story to the level of Mrs. Monroe's apartment in the second story is a distance of 32 feet perpendicular height. This, allowed 6½ inches to each step gives 60 steps which the Housekeeper must mount in order to receive orders from Mrs. Monroe. Of these 36 steps are between the drawing room and bed-chamber. If Mrs. Monroe receives morning visits, the fatigue she must undergo is easily imagined. . . . Therefore, at any Sacrifice, the Apartment of the family should be on the Principal floor.*

Latrobe especially disliked the plan of the main floor: "I will not enlarge upon that absurd hall of Entrance, which makes the house resemble a Polypus all Mouth. In the general plan of the house of the duke of Leinster, the entrance is on the Basement Story, into what is here a kitchen. This totally changes the effect of the distribution [of space]."[34]

The new domestic ideas of architecture and planning current in Europe seem to have been unknown to or dismissed by Hoban. His President's House could have been built in 1750 or even before, for all the innovation it projected. It was true that in terms of convenience Hoban's President's House was little more than a big cottage. Luxury was found in good-drawing fireplaces and paneled or louvered shutters, in cedar shavings packed beneath the floors and ceilings to thwart insects, and in structural ventilation sufficient to dry the house against humidity that made it rot and its air impure. Strong construction was an asset more readily understood than nuances of planning.

To further illustrate the difference between Hoban's old-fashioned ideas, really "givens" in what he built, and Latrobe's modern concepts, one can compare the sorts of everyday houses Hoban built to one Latrobe was to build for Commodore Stephen Decatur in 1819, across what is today Lafayette Park from the President's House. Hoban built many houses, including several on speculation to sell. Apparently they were all more or less alike, following the red-brick vernacular familiar all along the

East Coast, consisting of a central block of two or three stories, built up against the sidewalk, with a separate "ell" wing to the rear, connected or not, containing the kitchen and other work areas of the house.

The house Latrobe built for Commodore Decatur in 1819 rose only a few years after Hoban rebuilt the President's House. Commodore Decatur's house could hardly be more of a departure from this vernacular, though still designed to stand in marching order with the local row house tradition from the outside, virtually filling the city lot on which it stood. The kitchen was located not in a rear wing but on the ground floor of the main block in one of the two rooms that flanked the entrance. The house was built to be entered at ground level, the cellar wholly buried beneath it. The working area of the house was on the ground floor, its domestic spaces split by a formal entrance leading to a stair lobby that took one to the second floor's gala room, designed for entertaining. The third or chamber story held bedrooms. The zones for living were established in the arrangement of these upper stories.[35]

The contrast between the two types of houses defined the difference between the vernacular or traditional design of a builder and the design of an architect who tailored his plans to the specific needs of the client. This, according to modern thinking at the time, was the challenge of the architect: to build to fit, not merely to provide a familiar shell. It was a very advanced idea for American clients. In Latrobe's Decatur House plan one can analyze how Decatur advised his architect on the way he intended to use the house, whereas Hoban, for whom the President's House was probably the only nonvernacular structure he ever built, provided the space but with only a very occasional specification from a client for a particular off-beat exception—such as Washington's oval room.

THE PRESIDENT'S HOUSE OCCUPIED

Fourteen years passed from Adams's occupation of the White House to its destruction in the War of 1812. During that period alterations were made to the house. Some of the work was by Hoban and some by Latrobe, whose fees for the President's House were mostly buried in the much larger budget for the Capitol. Hoban built the principal stairs, but not before Jefferson had reconfigured them into a horseshoe design that allowed free visual passage through the house to the roofs of the long service wings that Latrobe built to the east and west of the original house. These followed Jefferson's own plan for concealing the domestic "offices" out of view, partially sunk on the north side and open to the warming and drying sunshine on the south. The cellars of the west service wing are today partially intact, with evidence of the ice and wine cellar built by Jefferson.

Hoban had lingering in his possession drawings he had made for President Washington for a portico on the north side. The long porch on the south side proposed in his early drawings had been postponed at some point not shown in the records. One can imagine President Washington wanting to approximate Mount Vernon's riverfront porch on the President's House, and likewise a lesser interest on the part of his successor. But one can stand on the South Lawn today and still see the cuts in the stone that would have received doors to a colonnaded porch.

Almost every president made changes to the White House. Adams wallpapered some of the rooms, but in most rooms the plaster was not dry enough to receive paper by the time he left. He ordered removal of the figures "of man or beast" George Andrews had placed on some of the mantels.[36] Adams further changed the main entrance to the house to the south from the front Hoban had designed. This reversal was probably to avoid entering the house over the deep areaway on the north, a hazard when crossed by a plain bridge of boards.

In addition to the two service wings, east and west, Jefferson and Latrobe also added a stone bridge supported by a groin vault on the north, to return the main entrance to that side. Latrobe wanted to do more and in 1807 did a plan for a remake of the main floor interior to reflect modern ideas of the sort described above—moving partitions, creating anterooms and a boudoir, and flattening out one end of President Washington's oval into a column screen. Perhaps Jefferson's White House called for too much use to allow such tearing up, or perhaps Jefferson's tastes were too archaic and French to bear Latrobe's British tastes.

Jefferson's changes were inventions for convenience. On Latrobe's advice, he added a fourth stair, one tucked away beneath the widened main stair to give a second vertical access to the hall outside the kitchen. The president had Hoban install an iron stove in one of the two basement kitchen fireplaces. Obtained in Baltimore, this "ranger" (it held a range of pots) was a modern adaptation built of iron plates, replacing the brick or stone "stew holes" that for at least a thousand years had served kitchens for cooking, fire safety, and greater economy in the use of fuel. The president further dispatched Hoban to Baltimore to purchase the parts of two water closets, one of which he installed at each end of the second floor, marking in 1801 the beginning of plumbing at the White House. These useful if unhealthy gadgets were fed from simple rain collection cisterns of tin, built into the attic and connected by a pipe to the water closet below, which resembled a pierced bench or chair. By pulling a cord or turning a crank, a gush of cistern-water was released through the bowl, carrying the waste down pipes in the walls of the house to rot in graveled sewers buried on the South Grounds.

President James Madison changed very little, but with his wife, Dolley, did permit Latrobe to introduce modern British Grecian decor to some rooms on the main floor, in spite of its very obvious bow to English taste. All of this met with torches from the British invaders on the stormy night of August 24–25, 1814.

THE WHITE HOUSE "REPAIRED"

All that was left of Hoban's White House were the stone walls and sections of their brick lining. Some of the brick vaulting had collapsed over the basement's cross hall. Most of the objects in the house were lost. Jefferson's iron kitchen range was dusted off, however, and returned to use. And in a pile of debris, Dolley Madison and Elizabeth Monroe saw large, broken pieces of mirrored glass from the oval room. They withdrew them from the pile and had them made into their own souvenirs as mirrored shaving stands.[37]

Despite the effort to move the capital farther west, to, say, Cincinnati with its river communication, President James Madison was solidly in support of keeping Washington as the capital, and he prevailed. Madison and Congress thus ordered the "repair" of the public buildings. Latrobe, falling on hard times, exerted himself trying to return to the job of federal architect, to rebuild and if necessary to redesign the incomplete Capitol and ruined President's House. He resurrected the plans with which he had hoped to woo Jefferson in 1807. Many improvements were presented, not least a revival of the portico on the north and a portico instead of a porch on the south. It was to no avail. Madison wanted the buildings "repaired," and Latrobe had not only proved himself difficult to deal with but wanted too many changes.

The president turned to the tried and true in appointing James Hoban to rebuild the President's House. He had built it once and could be relied upon to build it again as it had been, a decision politically inspired. The house was not entirely gone. About a third of the north wall remained, mostly the central part with the attached columns. All the walls of Collen Williamson's basement survived, and the stone walls of the South Front prevailed intact.

We have seen that the structure of the White House followed the modern custom of strengthening the external stone walls with soft brick. Earlier stone buildings and churches, such as Notre Dame in Paris, had been lined with wood. Brick was a shortcut as well as a method of fire prevention. The major destruction of the White House took place within the stone shell, where most of the brick had to be replaced. It had been a fire set and carried out in neat, emotionless military fashion: the kindling took place on the second or chamber floor, where a hot fire from smashed-up furniture and lamp oil quickly consumed the wooden attic structure above and with the resulting hellfire fell through the wooden timbers, flooring, and lath of the floor beneath, then crashed into the basement, where the eventual exhaustion of fuel and a fortuitous rain storm lowered and finally extinguished the fire. It was a fire both quick and neat, wholly businesslike.[38]

There was a lot left for Hoban to work with. He rebuilt the house and Jefferson's wings very much as they had been. Madison seems to have ordered few alterations, but after his Inauguration as president in March 1817, James Monroe did make changes. To the four corners of the chamber floor he added narrow rooms apparently as dressing rooms with the dual purpose of winter insulation for the adjacent large bedrooms, and one similar end room was added to the northwest corner room on the main floor as a pantry to serve what would always thereafter be a family or everyday dining room. Numerous fireplaces were added, all to burn coal and none to feature "nudities" in their ornaments.

The greatest change, it would seem, was in the architectural tone of the interior, but we know little about it, except for the result. As has been seen earlier, the original Hoban interior detailing appears to have been designed after mid-eighteenth-century tastes, while that of the rebuilt house was modern, in its openings trimmed simply, except for fancy wood corner blocks carved richly as rosettes with acanthus leaves. The walls were smooth plaster, intended for wallpaper or a popular rubbed-work finish known as "marble," rising to decorative cornices in cast plaster probably supplied by George Andrews. Marble mantelpieces were ordered for the State Rooms from a British agent in Leghorn, Italy. They arrived by sea, up the Chesapeake Bay and the Potomac River to Alexandria, then a part of the Federal District. One is in the Red Room today, and the other in the Green Room.

President Monroe was interested that the head of state be surrounded by ceremonial symbolism, conveyed by formal architecture and decorative art. While the pressure of his responsibilities necessitated the postponement of some of his ideas, he apparently had much more in mind than is documented. The East Room was not finished, although he approved and realized Hoban's design for handsome Grecian plaster decorations in a deep cornice of cast acanthus leaves, which were painted in silver leaf and backed by black cotton flocking. Short on funds, Monroe used the vast space to the degree that he was able to complete it. He ordered some seating furniture from a local cabinetmaker and, together with three iron candle chandeliers, probably forged in a blacksmith shop, rendered the room usable for the Marquis de Lafayette's visit in 1824. Beyond those improvements the East Room project was abandoned in that state, still incomplete.

HOBAN'S LAST WORK FOR THE PRESIDENTS

The first official use of the rebuilt house was on New Year's Day 1818, when President and Mrs. Monroe held the by now traditional reception, as well as, in the vaulted basement corridor, an open house for Hoban's workmen.

Hoban continued in business in Washington, largely building houses and serving in official positions in the city and the various organizations that had necessarily interested him. He seems always to have kept a profitable stock of rental property, advertising as early as 1805: "To be rented For one or more years, as may be agreed upon, the house at present by the subscriber fronting F Street north near the President's square, it contains four rooms with fire places, 2 garret rooms and a kitchen—on a lot immediately in the rear is a stable, carriage house, coal house and garden."[39] He kept the coals warm for federal work. He suffered personal loss in the early 1820s with the death of his wife Susana, followed by the deaths of his two daughters Catherine and Helen. The latter was remembered by the Italian sculptors working on the Capitol as a great beauty. The loss of his wife, two daughters, and an infant that had died at birth left Hoban a widower with seven living children, all of whom grew up as prominent citizens of Washington, notably the son of his same name, who became one of the outstanding lawyers of his day.

In 1824 President Monroe called Hoban to the White House to build a columned porch around the protruding bay made by the oval rooms on the South Front. This may well have been an idea of Jefferson's, turned over to Latrobe many years ago; it first appears as a concept in 1806 in one of Jefferson's many sketches for improvement of the President's House. To realize the original idea for a south porch, approved by President Washington, the addition of a stone podium was required, projecting entirely across the south wall of the basement as completed up to that time by Williamson, more than twenty years before. Perhaps as a way of saving money it was decided instead to wrap only the bow with a porch, extend its verticality with heroic columns, and discontinue the rest of the porch. Evidence of the original intent survives in the doorways still there today to give access to the parts of the porch never built but made into windows in-filled with "jib" doors that opened for special uses. Those serving the Blue Room, Green Room, and Red Room are used often, while those in the State Dining Room and East Room have grilles and can be opened as balconies.

From the podium Hoban extended eight tall Ionic composite columns, following the designs introduced to the White House as pilasters in the original construction. They contained full representations of the Double Scottish Rose on four corners of the capitals. The uninterrupted shafts of the columns are today altered by President Truman's 1952 balcony, which gave access to the second floor living quarters but was no improvement to Hoban's South Portico.

By 1824 times had changed, and so had the convenience of construction. Steam-cutting machines simplified creation of the column capitals, and steamboats transported the stone from the quarry. Aquia quarry's rich resource of sandstone was thinning, so Hoban familiarized himself with the rich Seneca quarry upriver and put it to use on the new South Portico. Alas, when dried it was a strong reddish color, quite in contrast to Aquia sandstone's soft pinkish tan.[40]

The stone walls had been whitewashed from the first to protect the nooks, crannies, and cracks in them from holding water and splitting in winter weather. When Hoban rebuilt and repaired the walls after the British burned the house, the soot stains were so impervious to lime washes that he covered the house with lead-based paint. Now seeing stone from the two quarries together was alarming, the contrast dashing the monolithic quality of the stonework. Hoban's solution was to continue with the lead paint. In so doing he willed a painted house to the future, one already in his time known as "The White House." The secrets of the original stone would not be revealed until well over a century had passed, when the old walls were stripped and repaired and painted again by the National Park Service in the 1980s and 1990s.[41]

The White House remained essentially as Hoban had improved it for President Monroe for five years. Congress held several bills that, if adopted and funded, would have carried the house to a semblance of completion and Hoban was standing by to do the work. He was at this time in his late 60s and still an active participant in business and the affairs of the city, serving as an elected alderman. He attended St. Patrick's Church, the Roman Catholic congregation for which he had built the brick church. He held his government jobs closely. Privately, James Monroe had called upon him to build his new country home, Oak Hill, in Loudoun County, Virginia, and Hoban did build the handsome columned house, seeing to the excellence of its brickwork—and to the use of discarded building materials from the President's House on the sly wherever possible. Mantels and even very likely the old roofing slate that had failed on the President's House roof seem to have found new homes in Oak Hill. Monroe never recorded his logic in justifying these borrowings, and Hoban remained silent, committed to pleasing him.[42]

It is likely that Charles Bulfinch, the government architect, provided the plans for Oak Hill, as he had for the expansion of St. John's Church on Lafayette Square across from the President's House. Observing the two buildings, one pauses over the classical similarity of the two facades. Bulfinch, a Boston architect famed and admired in New England, had impressed President Monroe with the beauty of his work, and Monroe was inspired to bring him to Washington. Hoban worked closely with Bulfinch on the completion of the north wing of the Capitol.

Monroe's successor, John Quincy Adams, was not so popular a president. His victory was suspect, the election thrown into the House of Representatives, and while he was outstanding in foreign relations, his one-term administration was clouded by true and imagined accusations of fraud. Nothing was done to the President's House during his term, though it was used heavily for entertaining and in that vein very popular.

The "landslide" that saw Andrew Jackson elected to the presidency in 1828 had immediate effects. Funding bills for the President's House were called up from dusty files and, amazingly, put into process even by some of Jackson's enemies, notably the venerable New York patroon General Stephen Rensselaer, an Adams supporter. As head of the congressional public buildings committee, Rensselaer requested after the election that Charles Bulfinch prepare a report by January 1829 on the government building projects outstanding. Working with Hoban, Bulfinch did produce the report, and work started before Jackson's Inauguration in March. The two projects were completion of the East Room and construction of the long-planned North Portico.[43]

Hoban's basic decorative work on the East Room had already been done, from the heavy anthem cornice to the wood wainscoting. All that was left with those elements was painting, gilding, and background flocking. Completion of the decorations was provided by Louis Veron & Co. of Philadelphia, which owned a one-stop luxury interior decoration "ware house" that provided all the elements of an interior from lighting to carpets. Andrew Jackson's friend and colleague Major William B.

Lewis of Tennessee made the contact and selections. The result can be likened to the most effusive hotel lobby, the colors yellow, royal blue, and gilt. Sumptuous would describe it best, from the three massive gilt oil-burning chandeliers, replacing those of iron, to the silk window hangings, to the huge "French plate" mirrors. An oval of gilded *papier-mâché* stars was glued over the arched doors to the room, to announce the entrance of the president.[44]

While the East Room involved Hoban only peripherally, perhaps with installation, its particular Jacksonian glory would pass with time. It was the addition of the North Portico that would permanently alter the architecture of the White House. We have seen how Hoban and Bulfinch took down Hoban's framed drawings for the portico from the wall in his house, and that Bulfinch traced them in preparing, presumably with Hoban, working drawings for the new portico, which Hoban built, beginning in 1829. He died in the Christmas season of 1831, and it may have still been under construction. Made entirely of stone, both Aquia and Seneca, with Ionic columns to match those on the South Portico,[45] it was more complicated to build than any other part of the house.

The North Portico was Hoban's last stroke on the building. It was both an architectural improvement and a practical porte cochere to keep the rain and snow away from the Front Entrance. But the appearance was more successful than mere protection from the weather. Bold yet not overbearing, the North Portico changed the image of the house, pushing to the rear the early Georgian detailing of Ireland and projecting a new sort of American idea, the columned porch. Few elements have so inspired American architecture, be it the august front of a bank or church or the embellishment of a simple box of a residence, from the plantation South to conservative New England. The portico assumed domination of the adapted Irish Leinster House that George Washington had approved forty years before and gave the President's House a quality easily seen as uniquely American, preparing it for the iconic role it was to serve in the centuries to come.

NOTES

1. Records for the building of the White House are found in Record Group 42, National Archives Building, Washington, D.C. They do not seem complete but are not sparse, containing bids for work, contracts, and references to plans, although few actual drawings. It is supposed that the many drawings James Hoban made or required for the work on the White House were used at the building site and worn out. The Records of the Commissioners for the District of Columbia are also in RG 42. After 1801 there was a single commissioner. Hoban is the focus of a special issue of *White House History*, no. 22 (Spring 2008).

2. *Philadelphia Post*, May 25, 1785.

3. The Purcells and Hobans were close and apparently interrelated with the Maryland family of Susana Sewall, later Hoban's wife. First names were repeated over the years in namesakes.

4. The Dublin Society medal and the medal for designing the White House are in the collections of the National Museum of American History, Smithsonian Institution, Washington, D.C.

5. The conveyance for selling Hoban's house in Charleston, dated January 13, 1798, can be found in the Charleston County Register of Deeds Office, bk. U6, pp. 231–32. Thanks to Nic Butler, Charleston County Public Library, for sharing this information. Apparently Hoban had built a second, better house on the same site. Thanks also to Denis Bergin of Charleston for this information and a snapshot of the home, now demolished. See also Denis Bergin, "James Hoban (1758–1831) of Desart and the District of Columbia," online at the Hibernofiles website, www.avergreen9.wixsite.com/hibernofiles; Nic Butler, "James Hoban's Charleston Home," *Charleston Time Machine*, Charleston County Public Library website, www.ccpl.org.

6. Richard Madden, *Catholics in South Carolina: A Record* (Lanham, Md.: University Press of America, 1985), 38–

42; Thomas F. Hopkins, "St. Mary's Church, Charleston, S.C.: The First Catholic Church in the Original Diocese of Charleston," *Year Book 1897, Charleston, South Carolina* (Charleston: Walker, Evans, & Cogswell, 1897), 434; Records of Federal Lodge No. 1, Washington, D.C.

7. See Jonathan H. Poston, *The Buildings of Charleston: A Guide to the City's Architecture* (Columbia, S.C.: University of South Carolina Press, 1997); Samuel Gaillard Stoney, *This Is Charleston: A Survey of the Architectural Heritage of a Unique American City* (Charleston: Carolina Art Association, 1944).

8. *New-York Magazine*, September 1792; *Charleston City Gazette*, August 9, 1792, and August 14, 1792; *New-York Mirror and Ladies' Literary Gazette*, August 23, 1828; Anna Wells Rutledge, *Artists in the Life of Charleston: Through Colony and State from Restoration to Reconstruction* (Philadelphia: American Philosophical Society, 1949), 148.

9. Warren L. Bingham, *George Washington's 1791 Southern Tour* (Charleston, S.C.: History Press, 2016).

10. *Charleston City Gazette and the Daily Advertiser*, August 9, 1792. See also George Washington to the Commissioners, Philadelphia, June 8, 1792, Commissioners, Letters Received, reprinted in *The Writings of George Washington Relating to the National Capital,* published in *Records of Columbia Historical Society* 17 (1914): 55–56, and available on *Founders Online* website, www.founders.archives.gov. See also "James Hoban, the Architect and Builder of the White House and the Superintendent of the Building of the Capitol at Washington," *American Catholic Historical Researches*, n.s. 3, no. 1 (January 1907): 35–52.

11. Proceedings, Commission of the Federal City, April 1791–October 1792; Thomas Jefferson to George Washington, March 11, 1791, in *Thomas Jefferson and the National Capital*, ed. Saul K. Padover (Washington, D.C.: U.S. Government Printing Office, 1946), 47–50. For the quarry and site work at the President's House, see William Seale, *A White House of Stone: Building America's First Ideal in Architecture* (Washington, D.C.: White House Historical Association, 2017), 4–10.

12. Daniel Carroll to Jacob Read, Washington, August 23, 1792, Commissioners, Letters Received.

13. George Washington to Commission, Charleston, May 17, 1791, in *The Writings of George Washington, 1748–1799*, ed. John C. Fitzpatrick (Washington, D.C.: U. S. Government Printing Office, 1931–44), 31:286; James Hoban to the Commissioners, December 1, 1792, Commissioners, Letters Received.

14. George Washington to the Commissioners, Philadelphia, June 8, 1792, Commissioners, Letters Received, available on *Founders Online* website, www.founders.archives.gov; Susan E. Smead, "Hoban's Design for the President's House" (MA thesis, University of Virginia, 1989).

15. Commissioners' Proceedings, March 22, 1792.

16. See Competition entries, Maryland Historical Society, Baltimore.

17. George Washington to the Commissioners, Philadelphia, June 8, 1792, Commissioners, Letters Received, available on *Founders Online* website, www.founders.archives.gov.

18. For Lord Edward, see Stella Tillyard, *Citizen Lord: The Life of Edward Fitzgerald, Irish Revolutionary* (New York: Farrar, Straus, and Giroux, 1998).

19. Commission Proceedings, March 14, August 11, September 22, 1793; James Hoban to the Commissioners, Proceedings, October 5, 1793, and Hoban to Commission, October 15, 1793; Commissioners, Letters Received; George Washington to the Commissioners, March 3, 1793, Commissioners, Letters Received. Washington selected the site personally. See his diary June 27–28, 1791, in *Writings of Washington Relating to the National Capital*, 27–28; Thomas Jefferson, draft for George Washington, "XIII: The Proclamation by the President," March 30, 1791, available on *Founders Online* website, www.founders.archives.gov.

20. Seale, *White House of Stone,* 6–10.

21. Commission to Mr. Johnson, Georgetown, August 8, 1792, and August 3, 1792, Commissioners, Letters Sent.

22. See Seale, *White House of Stone,* 11–13.

23. Agreement between Hoban and Henry Lee, December 12, 1793, Commissioners Proceedings, December 16–24, 1793.

24. Hoban to Commissioners, December 4, 1794.

25. Commission to George Budd, Washington, June 24, 1795, Commissioners, Letters Sent; *Alexandria Gazette,* March

14, 1793; Commission minutes, April 9, 1795.

26. William Seale, *The President's House: A History*, 2nd ed. (Washington, D.C.: White House Historical Association, 2008), 1:47.

27. Carpenters' Hall in described in a letter from Anthony Jerome to the Commissioners, June 10, 1800, Commissioners, Letters Received. It was a big, two story building, later abandoned and its wood stolen.

28. Commissioners to Hoban, July 31, 1793, Commissioners, Letters Received.

29. Commissioners to Harrison & Maynadier, Baltimore, October 15, 1799; Edward Langley, invoice for hardware from England, September 10, 1799, and Edward Langley to Commissioners, Commissioners, Letters Received.

30. See Abbie Rowe, photographs of the Truman renovation, 1948–52, National Archives.

31. Edward Lawler Jr., "George Washington's Bow Window: A Lost Fragment of White House Precedence Comes to Light in Philadelphia," *White House History,* no. 22 (Spring 2008): 58–61.

32. Hoban to the Commissioners, report, November 18, 1799–May 18, 1800.

33. Benjamin Henry Latrobe to William Lee, Washington, March 22, 1817, *The Correspondence and Miscellaneous Papers of Benjamin Henry Latrobe*, ed. John C. Van Horn and Lee W. Formwalt (New Haven: Yale University Press for the Maryland Historical Society, 1984–88), vol. 3.

34. Ibid.

35. For the Decatur House, see Michael Fazio, "A Rational House with Complications: Benjamin Henry Latrobe's Design," in James Tertius de Kay, Michael Fazio, Osborne Phinizy Mackie, and Katherine Malone-France, *The Stephen Decatur House: A History* (Washington, D.C.: White House Historical Association, 2018), 145–217.

36. Commissioners to George Andrews, November 1, 1800, Commissioners, Letters Sent.

37. Alexandra Parker, "Reflections After the Fire: The History of the Monroe Shaving Mirrors," *White House History,* no. 35 (Summer 2014): 102–05.

38. On the British invasion of Washington, see *America Under Fire: A Bicentennial Symposium* (Washington, D.C.: White House Historical Association, 2014).

39. *Washington Federalist,* March 16, 1805, 3–4.

40. Seale, *White House of Stone,* 42.

41. James I. McDaniel, "Stone Walls Preserved," *White House History,* no. 1 (1983): 38–45; Seale, *White House of Stone,* 122–33.

42. Unquestionably there is a story linking Oak Hill materially to the White House. Perhaps Monroe's universal popularity screened any questions the public had entertained. Oak Hill's borrowing are fairly clear, and it is an interesting house to study. The brickwork that surrounds the front door has a Hoban, even Dublin, quality, but the design of the house shows Charles Bulfinch's influence in the asymmetrical porch, one of the characteristics of the plan, more New England than traditional Virginia.

43. Seale, *President's House*, 1:168–69.

44. Louis Veron & Co. to Commissioner, November 25, 1829, Commissioner's miscellaneous Treasury warrants. See also Seale, *President's House*, 1:183–85.

45. Seale, *White House of Stone,* 116–21.

II. MERLO KELLY

The Building Line in Ireland

Gentlemen,

Being universally acquainted with men in the Building line in Ireland, particularly with many able Stone Cutters in Dublin with whom I have been concerned in building, as the Royal Exchange, New Bank, and Custom House, all of which buildings were done in the same stile as the business to be done here, and nearly the same kind of Stone, to these men I would write if it meets the approbations of the Commissioners, to embark for this City, early in the Spring, and hold out such terms to them as the Commissioners may think proper, and would recommend to engage them for two years, that the buildings may be done to a certainty, such hands have in Dublin a Guinea per week.[1]

In a letter dated November 3, 1792, James Hoban wrote to the Commissioners for the District of Columbia in Washington, D.C., outlining materials needed for construction of the President's House. He also promoted his connections with suitable stonemasons in Ireland and made reference to three buildings with which he had involvement—the Royal Exchange, the Newcomen Bank, and the Custom House. These significant buildings were pivotal in the context of architectural and urban development in late eighteenth-century Dublin, a period of transformative growth in the city. Hoban's formative years of training and apprenticeship in Dublin, and his involvement in such projects, undoubtedly prepared him for his illustrious career as an architect in the United States.

Hoban was born in 1755, and his childhood years were spent in Desart, Cuffesgrange, County Kilkenny. His father was a tenant farmer on the estate of the Cuffe family at Desart Court, a grand Palladian country house dating from 1733 and attributed to the acclaimed architect Edward Lovett Pearce. It was in the estate workshops at Desart Court that Hoban trained as a carpenter and wheelwright, until his move to Dublin in the 1770s, when the city was undergoing profound change.

Despite an emerging new architecture, and the construction of several buildings of significance in the first half of the eighteenth century, Dublin in mid-century retained the urban form of the medieval city, as is evident in an examination of John Rocque's 1756 map of Dublin. The formation of the Wide Streets Commission in 1757 signaled a turning point in the city's development—the start of a phase of enlightened planning and a radical reworking of the urban form. Initially set up to create a route from Capel Street to Dublin Castle, the Wide Streets Commission went on to become a hugely influential planning body in the development of the city. The commissioners were well traveled and well versed in contemporary urban developments in Europe and Great Britain. Many had embarked on a "Grand Tour" of Europe, bringing back with them new ideas about architecture and urban design. Their progressive thinking would have permeated architectural circles in Dublin and influenced attitudes to design, not least in the Dublin Society School of Architectural Drawing, where Hoban was a student.

It is often said that the legacy of this drawing school is immeasurable in that it shaped so many of the architects and craftsmen who designed and built the city of Dublin, not to mention those, like Hoban, who took their skills overseas. The school was established in 1750, when the Dublin Society (now the Royal Dublin Society) took over Robert West's school and appointed him master. West was an artist who had studied in Paris. Initially the focus was on figure drawing, with architectural, ornamental, and landscape drawing introduced later. The school was founded, according to John Turpin, because "Jean-Baptiste Descamps, founder of French art schools, influenced the Dublin Society with his ideas of providing free drawing education to craftsmen."[2]

The Dublin Society School of Architectural Drawing was founded in 1764 in Shaw's Court, and Thomas Ivory was appointed master. It may seem surprising that Ivory was given this appointment in the absence of any significant architectural projects to date. However, the architectural historian Edward McParland makes reference to the superb draftsmanship evident in Ivory's surviving drawings,[3] and these skills alone may explain why he was selected for the role. Ivory's disposition may also have influenced the appointment, and he is described as "a gentle urbane character" by J. D. Herbert, a former student in the school.[4] When Hoban attended the School of Architectural Drawing, it was based on Grafton Street, opposite the Provost's House in Trinity College and adjacent to the College Green. The objective of the school was advertised in *Faulkner's Dublin Journal* thus: "to teach twenty boys of a proper age and properly qualified, the principles of Geometry and the Elements of Architecture, and the Rules of Perspective, such boys being the children of indigent parents, under the care and tuition of Mr. Ivory who has the liberty also to take in scholars for his own benefit."[5]

About thirty to thirty-five pupils attended the drawing school each year, and the architectural historian Maurice Craig claims that "there was not a working tradesman or mechanic in the building line in Dublin and the chief towns in Ireland who, during his apprenticeship, had not received instruction in it."[6] It is worthy of note that from 1749 to 1849, like the French model, tuition at the school was free, and this made the school accessible to all tiers of society. The practical nature of the courses made them attractive to artisans and craftsmen. However, despite the emphasis on practical skills, Turpin writes that the teaching ethos at the school elevated the level of architectural training from the intricacies of construction techniques to a more intellectual plane.[7] There was also the prospect of travel and further studies abroad, advantages that may have appealed to the young Hoban. According to Walter D. Strickland,

> *The pupils, who had to be under fourteen years of age, were admitted free to one or all of the schools; examinations were held yearly and medals and money-prizes awarded. In the case of promising pupils the Society encouraged and helped them, sometimes paying for their apprenticeship, or giving them an allowance for their clothing and maintenance, and occasionally enabling them to go to London or to Italy for further study.*[8]

The study of geometry and perspective were central to the curriculum, reflecting traditional Renaissance design principles. The students studied plans and elevations of important architectural works and produced detailed measured drawings. They also devised their own designs to briefs set out by Ivory, and prizes were awarded for merit by the Dublin Society. James Gibbs's *Rules for Drawing the Several Parts of Architecture* (1736), Sir William Chambers's *Treatise on Civil Architecture* (1759), and Andrea Palladio's *Four Books of Architecture* (1570; complete English ed., 1715–20) were among the seminal texts prescribed for the students. There were also a number of more practical manuals such as Francis Price's *British Carpenter* (1759) and William Halfpenny's *Modern Builder's Assistant* (1742). Turpin observes that the selected books and publications reflect Ivory's conservative taste and his training as a carpenter, for they were "by no means au courant with Neo Classicism."[9]

The School of Ornament Drawing was also open to the students of the School of Architectural Drawing, allowing them the opportunity to study the classical vocabulary of decorative ornament for interiors. Thus the students were exposed to an extensive range of architectural precedents, from antique Roman engravings to the latest international eighteenth-century designs in Ireland and abroad. This training was intended to equip students for their practice. In May 1772, the Dublin Society ruled that "no person shall be admitted as a scholar into the School for Drawing in Architecture . . . who is not intended to follow some business wherein a knowledge of Architecture is necessary."[10] This ethos was further compounded by the requirement that students gain practical experience working with architects during their time in the school. The premium system, of which Hoban was a beneficiary, served as a reference for potential employers.

In addition to James Hoban, some notable architects who passed through the school were Francis Sandys, Richard Morrison, Robert Pool, and John Cash. Pool and Cash's 1780 *Views of the Most Remarkable Public Buildings, Monuments and Other Edifices in the City of Dublin* was patronized by the Dublin Society and included written descriptions of the buildings in addition to measured drawings. Desmond Guinness, who co-founded the Irish Georgian Society with Mariga Guinness in 1958, highlights the significance of the Pool and Cash engravings:

> *The engravings of Pool and Cash were the nearest approach to a* Vitruvius Hibernicus *that was ever published. On occasion the authors must have had access to architectural plans that have since disappeared, and they record therefore the architect's intentions rather than the building itself. In most cases, however, they are extremely accurate, and there is a pristine elegance and clarity in their engraving that makes them unique.*[11]

Ivory was head of the School of Architectural Drawing until his death at the end of 1786. In 1787, Henry Aaron Baker, a pupil of James Gandon, was appointed head and remained in that position until his death in 1836. Without doubt, Hoban's training in the drawing school and his practice as a carpenter and draftsman would have introduced him to some influential figures in Dublin building circles in addition to Ivory, master of the school and respected architect. Hoban's involvement in noteworthy architectural projects at the time, alluded to in his written correspondence with the Commissioners for the District of Columbia, Washington, is testament to this.

The Royal Exchange, now the City Hall, was designed by a young English architect, Thomas Cooley, following a competition in 1768. James Gandon, architect of the Custom House, placed second, and Thomas Ivory, architect of the Newcomen Bank, was first among the Irish entries. The Royal

Exchange was the first large-scale neoclassical building in Ireland, and its construction marked a significant turning point in Dublin's architectural trajectory. It was described by Christine Casey in her Pevsner guide to the architecture of Dublin as "the harbinger of Dublin's superlative civic architecture of the late eighteenth century."[12] Cooley's building was constructed between 1769 and 1779 and formed part of the aforementioned route between Capel Street and Dublin Castle.

The Custom House was the work of James Gandon, and its siting formed part of one of the greater visions that the Wide Streets Commission had for the city. The proposal for a new Custom House was not without controversy, representing an eastern expansion from the medieval city core. The existing Custom House was situated on the quays near Dublin Castle and the Royal Exchange, in the heart of the historic city. The proposed location for the new Custom House on the northeastern quays was of particular strategic interest to several members of the Wide Streets Commission who were instrumental in the eastern urban expansion and had private concerns in its development. There was such opposition to this project, which consolidated the eastward shift, that Gandon reputedly received threatening letters and was known to carry "a good cane sword" to the site.[13] Completed between 1781 and 1791, Gandon's Custom House is considered a masterpiece of European neoclassicism, embodying the optimistic aspirations of late eighteenth-century Ireland.

The "New Bank" Hoban alludes to in his letter is the Newcomen Bank, designed by Thomas Ivory and referred to in the 1793 *Anthologia Hibernica* as "Sir Wm. Newcomen's new bank in Dublin."[14] Ivory was commissioned to design a bank and private residence for Sir William Gleadowe-Newcomen in 1778. The Royal Exchange was nearing completion, and the area around Castle Street had emerged as a banking quarter. It was within this context that Ivory was given a complex corner site at the junction of Castle Street and Cork Hill, opposite the Royal Exchange and the entrance to Dublin Castle, on which to design his building.

As Hoban does not clarify his exact involvement in these three projects, we are left to speculate in this regard. We know that as part of their training, students in the School of Architectural Drawing were obliged to gain professional experience by working with practicing architects. Hoban may have been an apprentice to Thomas Ivory. Originating from Cork, Ivory, like Hoban, began life as a carpenter. He spent time in the workshop of a gunsmith before training under a "Mr Bell Mires"[15] and establishing his practice in Dublin as a draftsman and architect. As the master of the drawing school could "take in scholars for his own benefit," given that Ivory was master of the school and that his student Hoban was awarded second prize for "Drawings of Brackets, Stairs, Roofs &c." in November 1780, it is plausible that Ivory would have engaged him as an apprentice.

The Newcomen Bank has been widely celebrated for the skill with which it was composed and constructed. Casey describes the building as an "enigmatic and exquisitely made building."[16] The facade compositions, with shallow relieving arches and spare niches, reference the work of the architects Robert and James Adam in London, prompting Craig to describe the bank as "the only building in Dublin which looks as though it might have been designed by one of the Adams."[17]

Ivory's building, which was later extended, comprised a three-room plan with a central top-lit open-well stair hall. This elegant space features delicate plasterwork similar to the work of Charles Thorp in the Royal Exchange, and a cantilevered stone staircase with a decorative wrought-iron balustrade. Newcomen Bank was designed as a private banking house and residence. The first floor oval room, with views of the Royal Exchange and the entrance to Dublin Castle, was likely to have been

Newcomen's principal bank parlor, where he would have welcomed select clients. This delightful room features a trompe l'oeil ceiling that has been attributed to the Italian painter Vincent Waldré; it depicts cherubs bearing flowers and wreaths against the backdrop of a clouded sky. The walls of the former bank parlor are expressed as a blind arcade incorporating doors, windows, and storage recesses, with fine joinery details. If Hoban was involved in the construction of the project, it is likely that his role was as a carpenter, and perhaps as a draftsman. And though the ingenious use of the oval in the plan form was driven by the confined plot, it is interesting to reflect on the oval room as a predecessor of Hoban's later creation in his designs for the President's House in Washington.

The fine carving on the facade of the bank is the work of Simon Vierpyl, an acclaimed sculptor and stonemason of Dutch origins who had learned his trade in London. As a young stonemason, Vierpyl had spent nine years in Rome, where he was engaged in making copies of sculptures for "Grand Tourists." Lord Charlemont encountered him while on his "Grand Tour" and invited him to Dublin to supervise construction on the exquisite Casino at Marino, designed by Sir William Chambers. Vierpyl arrived in Dublin in 1756 and was responsible for decorative carvings on several prominent buildings in the city, including the Newcomen Bank, the Royal Exchange, Charlemont House, and the Blue Coat School. According to the *Dictionary of Irish Architects*, "He was chiefly engaged in building-related activities, as stonecarver and mason, as clerk of works and as a speculative developer."[18]

Vierpyl's involvement on the Newcomen Bank and the Royal Exchange would suggest that he may be one of the stonecutters that Hoban references in his letter. In addition, Vierpyl's protégé Edward Smyth was the principal stonemason on Gandon's Custom House. Smyth went on to become master of the Dublin Society School of Modelling and Sculpture. To complete the circle, Gandon and Vierpyl were also involved in the Dublin Society School of Architectural Drawing and Hoban would undoubtedly have crossed paths with them during his time there.

The documentation of Hoban in Irish archival repositories is scant, and so a further exploration of the workings of contemporary stonecutters such as Vierpyl and Smyth may allow insights into the exact nature of Hoban's involvement in the Dublin scene. If, indeed, Vierpyl is one of the stonecutters referred to by Hoban, as their collective catalog of works would suggest, then his engagement in speculative building work is of interest. Vierpyl is documented in archival leases to have owned and developed plots in Parnell Square, Henry Street, Granby Row, Cullen's Place, William Street South, Bachelors Walk, and the North Wall. The construction process at that time in Dublin was a collaborative one, and given Hoban's claim to be "universally acquainted with men in the Building line in Ireland" and in particular stonecutters, he may well have acted as draftsman for Vierpyl in his private projects.

On reflection, Hoban's training at the Dublin Society School of Architectural Drawing not only gave him the skills to practice as an architect but opened the doors to an influential circle of developers, architects, and craftsmen who helped consolidate his architectural training before he left for America. Perhaps he had this in mind when he established his drawing school in Charleston in 1790, advertising a recommendation from the Dublin school, "one of the first academies of arts and sciences in Europe."[19]

NOTES

This essay is based on the author's presentation at the White House Historical Association symposium "The United Kingdom and Ireland in the White House: A Conversation on Historical Perspectives," Washington, D.C., April 17, 2018.

1. James Hoban to the Commissioners for the District of Columbia, Washington, November 3, 1792, Records of the Commissioners for the District of Columbia, Record Group 42, Letters Received, National Archives, Washington, D.C.
2. John Turpin, *A School of Art in Dublin Since the Eighteenth Century* (Dublin: Gill & Macmillan, 1995).
3. Edward McParland, *Thomas Ivory, Architect* (Dublin: Gifford and Craven, 1973), 2.
4. J. D. Herbert, *Irish Varieties, for the Last Fifty Years* (London: W. Joy, 1836), 57.
5. *Faulkner's Dublin Journal*, February 10, 1764.
6. Maurice Craig, *Dublin, 1660–1960* (Dublin: Allen Figges, 1969), 122.
7. Turpin, *School of Art in Dublin*.
8. "The Dublin Society" in Walter G. Strickland, *A Dictionary of Irish Artists* (Dublin: Maunsel & Company, 1913), 2:582, available online at www.libraryireland.com.
9. Turpin, *School of Art in Dublin*.
10. Ibid.
11. Desmond Guinness, introduction to *Limited Edition of Georgian Dublin Plates from Original Engravings by Pool and Cash 1780* (Castletown: Irish Georgian Society, 1971).
12. Christine Casey, *Dublin: The City Within the Grand and Royal Canals and the Circular Road with the Phoenix Park*, Pevsner Architectural Guides (New Haven: Yale University Press, 2005), 361.
13. Constanina Maxwell, *Dublin Under the Georges, 1714–1830* (Dublin: Lanby Books, 1997), 55.
14. *Anthologia Hibernica*, May 1793, 334–35, copy in National Library of Ireland, Dublin.
15. "Mr Bell Mires" has been identified by Frederick O'Dwyer as the surveyor, measurer. and topographical draftsman Jonas Blaymire (d. 1763). See entry in Strickland, *Dictionary of Irish Artists*, 1:68–69.
16. Casey, *Dublin*, 365.
17. Craig, *Dublin*, 220.
18. "Simon Vierpyl," in Strickland, *Dictionary of Irish Artists*, 2:488–90.
19. "Architecture," advertisement by Hoban & Purcell, *Charleston City Gazette,* April 17, 1790.

III. FINOLA O'KANE

Eighteenth-Century Irish Landscape Design and Its Translation to America by James Hoban

James Hoban's spatial education began in the countryside of County Kilkenny, where he learned to read the patterns of the Irish landscape and its architecture. Hoban was born the son of Edward Hoban and Martha Bayne Hoban in 1755. His father was reputedly a tenant farmer on the Cuffe estate in this rich, long-settled inland county of Ireland, where Norman patterns of enclosure and landholding were well established. Structured into manors, the centerpiece of each manor was the lord's house, often known as the "great house" or "big house" in Ireland. It was surrounded by its *demesne* land—an old Norman word denoting the land held and farmed by the landlord himself (pages 92–93). Typically located where the land was richest and most productive, demesne land generally avoided areas that were poor or low lying, such as boglands, heaths, moors, or marshes. Beyond the demesne land lay the tenants' holdings, typically grouped into fields connected by walls, paths, and *boreens* or small roads. Each tenant's acreage was recorded in the landlord's book of leases, together with how much rent he or she paid and when. All the tenants typically paid their rents on "gale days," usually at six-month intervals, and a special room for the landlord or his agent to receive such rents was accommodated into the design of many country houses.

The great house of Desart Court (demolished in the 1950s) was built and owned by the Cuffe family, descended from Captain Joseph Cuffe, a seventeenth-century soldier in Oliver Cromwell's army and, according to the official history, the "recipient of one of the largest Cromwellian land grants in Co. Kilkenny, over 3,500 acres."[1] His grandson John Cuffe, created first Baron Desart in 1733, built Desart Court (page 89) in the early 1730s, with its design attributed to Edward Lovett Pearce, one of Ireland's most distinguished architects. The family's elevation to the peerage probably inspired the construction of a new and more impressive house than the older Castle Inch, Captain Joseph's house, and its formal walled gardens, the ruins of which still stand some 3 miles north of Desart Court's now lost mansion (pages 98–99).

For country houses, the family's property footprint usually left the choice of orientation almost entirely at the designer's discretion, unlike an urban or suburban commission that had to take its surroundings closely into account. Desart Court enjoyed an east-west orientation that allowed its garden front to benefit from the evening sun and views westward. Its farm buildings and walled gardens were grouped north of the house—a most satisfactory solution, preventing them from blocking the designed vistas that lay east, south, and westward. Nor did they interfere with the approach routes that stemmed from the major roads leading to Callan and Kilkenny. Two formal entrance routes were laid out to wind agreeably toward the house, one from the northeast and another from the south. By the mid-eighteenth century, and certainly by the time of Hoban's birth in 1755, any axial or orthogonal design features such as avenues, parterres, canals, ponds, or fountains were likely to have been swept away by the growing popularity of Lancelot ("Capability") Brown's landscape design, which was characterized by a high stone boundary wall, a tree belt of great broadleaf species to encircle the demesne, curvilinear approach routes for viewing from a carriage, and undulating grassy parkland, dotted with clumps and specimen trees. In the absence of any eighteenth-century demesne plans of Desart Court, such features are visible on the c. 1837 1st edition Ordnance Survey map and are likely to have been in train during Hoban's youth and adolescence. When compared with architecture, eighteenth-century landscape design had a very long gestation period, with its full maturity rarely, if ever, appreciated by those who planted it. Yet it is this strategic quality—its belief in future rather than immediate beauty—that lends it such ingenuity and longevity.

The Cuffe family's new aristocratic status was reflected in the ambition of Desart Court's eighteenth-century landscape design, possibly more so than its house.[2] The elements that most betray this ambition are the deer park and the Greatwood that still exist northward to westward of it. Deer parks spoke of medieval lineage, noble blood, and an ancient right to the soil that the high fence or wall enclosed so carefully, and such symbols were valuable in Ireland, particularly for families, such as the Cuffes, who were seventeenth-century arrivistes. Commoners were not entitled to hunt or eat venison, and a deer park carved out a particular distinction for any noble family, particularly so in Ireland of the early eighteenth century, when many of the nobility, whether *nouveau* or *ancien*, found such landscapes useful for legitimizing their ascendancy.[3] The gentleman's park, origin and touchstone of the landscape garden, adopted much of its seemingly casual aesthetic from the medieval environs of the deer park. The plan of the 1842 Ordnance Survey map suggests that the Greatwood was once laid out as a *forêt ornée* (pages 92–93). This was a style of planting that used the *in utile dolce* concept beloved of early eighteenth-century improvers. The trees were grown for their wood but were laid out in agreeable walks and allées where riders (more than strollers) could enjoy the long avenues undulating agreeably over Ireland's not-so-flat countryside. This style was introduced to Ireland by Stephen Switzer, who advised on aspects of the landscape design for Castletown House, County Kildare, at the invitation of Speaker William Conolly of the Irish House of Commons. Edward Lovett Pearce may have become acquainted with Switzer's work during his own involvement in the design of Castletown House.[4]

Irish landowners, typically poorer than their English counterparts, often did not have the wherewithal to build very large houses or to lay out very grand parklands, and Irish Palladian houses were often smaller and less grandiose than those of England as a consequence. This situation had the benefit of ensuring that Irish country houses and demesnes often came close to the true Palladian ideal—a self-sufficient farm and farmhouse where its owner was intimately engaged in such pursuits as improving the soil, following best farming practice, whether arable, pastoral, or mixed, and generally extending benevolence to tenants and the wider community. This middle size was easier to translate to the United States, whose Founding Fathers also prided themselves on their modest self-sufficiency and lack of ostentation and unnecessary expense. The general eighteenth-century ideology of agricultural improvement and its positive benefits are particularly evident in such relatively wealthy counties as County Kilkenny, where the more problematic characteristics of the Irish countryside, namely poverty, sectarian division, and colonial superiority of newcomers over natives, were less in evidence than in other parts of Ireland. The United States was also given to agricultural improvement, with such Founding Fathers as George Mason, George Washington, and Thomas Jefferson acting as its leading American exponents. James Hoban, a child of improved Kilkenny farmland, would have found it very easy to adapt its principles to the rich soils of South Carolina and the inlets of the Potomac.

Other country houses from Pearce's portfolio that bear comparison with the design and scale of Desart Court include the Bishop's Palace, Cashel (1730–32), and Bellamont Forest, County Cavan (1730). Neighboring great houses, with which Hoban was probably familiar, include Castle Inch (page 99), Westpark, Callan House, Grange House (also occupied by the Cuffe family), and Castletown Cox. Constructed in the late 1760s, Castletown Cox was the apex of Irish country house design in the years immediately preceding Hoban's departure for America in the early 1780s (page 100).[5] Located some 18 miles due south of Desart Court, it was Davis Ducart's masterwork, constructed c. 1767, and it seems unlikely that an ambitious young architect would not have known of it.[6] Of a scale similar to that of Desart Court, Castletown Cox enjoys a similar seven bay over basement Palladian composition, an northeast-southwest orientation, and one-story wings that surround a rectangular entrance courtyard (page 102). But Castletown Cox was built for an untitled family and was surrounded by a smaller demesne that Desart Court's. Its landscape design suggested the Cox family's lesser landholding and social status: it has no deer park, no consistent tree belt, fewer approach routes, less park land, and far more bounded and named fields (page 101).[7] Such exact design distinctions, expressive of a family's status, taste, and wealth, and their confidence and expectations in such arenas, would have been very intelligible to an Irish architect such as James Hoban.

In his teenage years Hoban moved to Dublin. The eighteenth century was a golden era of expansion and prosperity for Dublin as it grew to become the second city of the British Empire and the sixth largest city in Europe, reaching a population of 200,000 by 1800.[8] Edel Sheridan-Quantz has described its transformation over the course of the early eighteenth century as one "from a relatively compact single-centred walled town with incipient suburbs to what was by the standards of the time a metropolis."[9] The young Hoban learned his profession in the midst of a building boom, when property developers vied with each other, said one, to "catch at and conclude bargains while People [were] in the Mind, & not give them time to cool or reflect."[10] Unlike comparable property portfolios in London, Edinburgh, or Bath, success was achieved on low-lying, reclaimed, and seaside land, requiring exceptional ingenuity in both finance and marketing in order to do so. This freewheeling and entrepreneurial environment may have served Hoban well in the young cities of the United States.

James FitzGerald, later Earl of Kildare and then Duke of Leinster, Ireland's premier nobleman, had made the first design commitment to a sea prospect in 1741 when he commissioned Richard Castle to build what was first known as Kildare House and subsequently as Leinster House and now the Dáil, the Republic of Ireland's Parliament House, with its garden front turned toward a sea vista. This commitment was relatively shortsighted in that Kildare did not own the entire site upon which he built his townhouse; its garden was owned by the viscounts, and it was their property developments that fixed the eastern bias of Dublin city and confirmed that of its northern quarter also. The development of these low-lying eastern areas by predominantly genteel housing developments gave Dublin an unusual structure. In direct contrast to both London and Paris, Dublin's wealthy lived close to the sea and docks, and the east end of Dublin gradually became the preferred end of town. In their 1780 book on Dublin, Robert Pool and John Cash remarked with some surprise: "It is here necessary to remark, that the eastern side of the City, contiguous to the sea, is almost entirely laid out in elegant streets, for the residence of the gentry: and the western side, though more remote from the sea, and consequently not so conveniently situated for the purposes of commerce, is chiefly inhabited by merchants and mechanicks."[11]

Dublin's swivel to the sea was also indebted to the city's growing pride in its maritime identity. As a port city, Dublin drew comparative inspiration from the other great port cities of Europe, particularly Amsterdam, the richest and most successful trading city of the seventeenth-century North Atlantic. Richard Castle, architect of many of Ireland's mid-century country houses, recommended his talents to Irish gentlemen by referring almost exclusively to the knowledge he had acquired from Dutch projects and sources.[12] Castle's design for Kildare House, later known as Leinster House, exploited the site's interstitial, suburban character. Its entrance front was clearly in the city, drawn from the tradition of the French hotel (page 149), while its garden front affected the character and setting of a country house. Drawings and paintings of the east-facing garden front depict the house standing in Platonic perfection, free from any service wings and framed by luxurious shrubberies (page 148). Probably positioned so that its residents could enjoy vistas of the ships entering Dublin Bay, this eastern prospect embraced the River Dodder's confluence with the Liffey, the fields of Baggots Rath, the strand of Merrion, and the Irish Sea (page 146). James Hoban's design for the world's most famous house has a similar Janus-like quality, with one face to the city and Pennsylvania Avenue and the other toward its garden, the public park that became the National Mall, the distant Potomac, and the sea.

When Hoban traveled across the Atlantic Ocean to his new homeland of the United States, the young country's spatial and social characteristics must have appeared both strange and familiar. American town plans were not born of old medieval manors, fields, lanes, roads, and pathways. Yet the young Washington, D.C., like the many Irish estate towns and areas of Dublin that were laid out in the eighteenth century, followed clear classical and rectilinear precepts. Hoban's clients in America were likely to be self-made men along the lines of Joseph Cuffe, ancestor of John Cuffe, his father's landlord. Men such as George Washington wrote and corresponded with such eighteenth-century Irishmen, perhaps acknowledging in doing so that America was more like Ireland than it was like England. Ireland was a country where frontier battles had recently been fought and where many successful men had not inherited vast ancestral estates from distant ancestors. It is not by chance that it was to just such a man and house in north Dublin that Washington wrote when describing the lifestyle and ambience he hoped to create at Mount Vernon, his "retreat from the cares of public life; where in homespun and with rural fare, we will invite you to our bed & board."[13] This self-sufficient, modest, and humble lifestyle was considered to embody all that European aristocratic life did not, and George Washington found Belcamp, and its owner-builder Edward Newenham, a model Irish version of country house design:

> *The manner in which you employ your time at Bell champ (in raising nurseries of fruit, forest trees, and shrubs) must not only contribute to your health & amusement, but it is certainly among the most rational avocations of life for what can be more pleasing, than to see the work of ones own hands, fostered by care and attention, rising to maturity in a beautiful display of those advantages and ornaments which by the Combination of Nature and taste of the projector in the disposal of them is always regaling and at the sametime in their seasons they are grateful to the palate.*[14]

James Hoban, born and raised in Kilkenny, and educated in Dublin, took his understanding of Irish landscape and architecture with him to the United States. This essay has set out to suggest where Hoban's understanding was acquired and how its translation encouraged a sympathy and appreciation of both countries in its designer, to the ongoing benefit of all American and Irish citizens today.

NOTES

1. "Agmondisham Cuffe," in *History of the Irish Parliament, 1692–1800*, ed. Edith May Johnston-Liik (Belfast: Ulster Historical Foundation, 2002), 3:557.

2. John Bateman, *The Great Landowners of Great Britain and Ireland* (London: Harrison and Sons, 1878), 114. By 1878 the Earls of Desart (the Cuffes had been further ennobled to an earldom in 1793) had an estate of 8,000 acres in Kilkenny and 932 acres in County Tipperary, with the Kilkenny portion valued at £5,778, a high value per acre when compared with the land of such counties as Galway, Kerry, or Wicklow, where the land was mostly of poorer quality.

3. In a competitive assessment of the ancient woodland of Castletown, Emily Lennox, wife of James FitzGerald and later Duchess of Leinster, bemoaned the strange lack of such woodland in her new home of Carton in 1762: "It's a pity us poor invalids have not such a one; I hope that is not coveting one's neighbour's goods." Emily FitzGerald (née Lennox), twentieth Countess of Kildare, later first Duchess of Leinster, to James FitzGerald, twentieth Earl of Kildare, later first Duke of Leinster, December 2, 1762, *Correspondence of Emily, Duchess of Leinster,* ed. Brian Fitzgerald (Dublin: Irish Manuscripts Commission, 1949), 1:145.

4. See Finola O'Kane, *Landscape Design in Eighteenth-Century Ireland: Mixing Foreign Trees with the Natives* (Cork: Cork University Press, 2004), chap. 2, for more on Switzer's design involvement at Castletown.

5. Patrick M. Geoghegan, "James Hoban," in *Dictionary of Irish Biography,* Cambridge University Press, www.dib.cambridge.org. Hoban advertised his services in Philadelphia in 1785.

6. Desmond Guinness and William Ryan, *Irish Houses and Castles* (London: Thames and Hudson, 1980), 219.

7. Bateman, *Great Landowners of Great Britain and Ireland*, 399. The Cox family estate totaled 4,581 acres, of which only 2,790 acres were located in County Kilkenny. The entire estate produced a rent roll of £3,133. See also 1st ed. Ordnance Survey map of Castletown Cox demesne, County Kilkenny, c. 1837.

8. J. Bradford DeLong and Andrei Shleifer, *Princes and Merchants: European City Growth Before the Industrial Revolution*, February 1993, NEBR Working Paper w4274, SSRN website, www.ssrn.com.

9. Edel Sheridan-Quantz, "The Multi-Centred Metropolis: The Social Topography of Eighteenth-Century Dublin," in *Two Capitals: London and Dublin, 1500–1840*, ed. Peter Clark and Raymond Gillespie (Oxford: British Academy for Oxford University Press, 2001), 287.

10. William Fitzwilliam, Dublin, to his brother the Rt. Hon. Viscount Fitzwilliam, Jermyn St., St. James, September 28, 1752, Pembroke Estate MSS, box 97/46/1/2/7/3, National Archives of Ireland, Dublin.

11. Robert Pool and John Cash, *Views of the Most Remarkable Public Buildings, Monuments and Other Edifices in the City of Dublin* (Dublin: J. Williams, 1780), 14.

12. Richard Castle, "An Essay on Artificial Navigation," c. 1730, MS 2737, National Library of Ireland, Dublin.

13. George Washington, Mount Vernon, to Sir Edward Newenham, Bell Champ, near Dublin, June 10, 1784, available on *Founders Online* website, www.founders.archives.gov. In his excellent book *The Pleasure Gardens of Virginia: From Jamestown to Jefferson* (Princeton: Princeton University Press, 1991), Peter Martin mistakenly located "Bell Champ" in England (p. 144), leading many to underestimate the connections between the historic landscape at Belcamp and Mount Vernon in Virginia. See also Finola O'Kane, "Designs for Belcamp and Mount Vernon," *Irish Georgian Society Review,* November 2017, 16–19, online at Irish Georgian Society website, www.igs.ie.

14. George Washington, Mount Vernon, to Sir Edward Newenham, April 20, 1787, available on *Founders Online* website, www.founders.archives.gov.

IV. CHRISTOPHER MORAN

Life as Lived in Irish Country Houses: Desart Court and Leinster House

It may surprise some visitors to Washington, D.C., that the architect of the White House, located in the heart of the bustling American capital, spent his formative years and early apprenticeship in the bucolic Irish countryside. But upon closer study of this most iconic building, it is clear that not only did the heyday of country life in grand country houses on the island of Ireland influence the architectural style of young James Hoban, but that the White House has, throughout its life, functioned much like a grand Irish country house itself—both as a seat of power and as an evolving country home.

Standing with its front portico facing Lafayette Park—as tourists gather for photographs and people from all walks of life meander the crisscross of pathways under magnolia trees—sits the graceful building that could be described as a grand country house, the White House, a home for the American family.

HISTORY

James Hoban spent his boyhood in County Kilkenny, Ireland, in a tenant house on the Desart estate owned by the noble Cuffe family. The largest landholdings, families, and estates on the island stood tall and grand—Carton House, Leinster House, Powerscourt House, Lough Glynn House, Portumna Castle, Rockingham House, and Desart—to name a few. The mansions upon these estates had been heavily influenced by architects from Britain and the Continent to accommodate and display the extravagant lifestyles, travels, and accomplishments of their patrons. Traces of Italian and French architecture were purposefully selected to speak to their occupants' knowledge, breadth of international importance, style, and power, and to impress.

Building projects across the island of Ireland had flourished in the eighteenth and nineteenth centuries, as, indeed, life in Irish country houses was uniquely shaped by lives in cities. As early as the fourteenth century, the influences of the Continent had begun to shape the tastes of the elite on the island, who requested architects from Germany, England, and Italy to build both their city and their countryside manors. Architects and estate owners gradually began to depart from the cold, deterring strongholds, castles, and defense-like structures of the Normans. In the seventeenth century, as travel became more accessible and landowners were able to increase rents more easily, life within country houses dictated successive remodels and iterations on facades. These grand houses grew and changed to display a welcoming warmth for growing families. The grand Irish country house beckoned to important visitors, accommodated an increasing number of heirs and teams of servants, demonstrated its families' influence or aspirations, and allowed owners to periodically enjoy the retreat and pleasures of the fields and open air.

Desart Court would have been a recurring and important sight for young Hoban while a boy sketching on paper and honing his penchant for design. Built over 1733, Desart Court, part of the family seat, was a relatively new and distinguished Palladian structure said to have been designed by Edward Lovett Pearce, who also designed Parliament House (Tithe na Parlaiminte). It was one of the first large estate houses erected on the island of Ireland during the building boom of the eighteenth century.

John Cuffe, the first Lord Desart in the Irish House of Lords, and Otway Cuffe, an Anglo-Irish peer and lawyer who succeeded him, invested a large part of the family fortune over several years in ensuring Desart's place in history. The interior of Desart Court boasted pictures by Old Masters, dado wood paneling, rococo ceilings, bookcases "enriched in fluted pilasters,"[1] woodwork, and tapestries. To the Desart family, the building was intended to look formidable and stand out against the countryside, just as they desired their family to do. Wrote a frequent visitor, Dorothea Herbert, the granddaughter of the first Lord Desart:

> *We went to Desart, Lord Desart's fine old family Seat in the County Kilkenny remarkable for its fine Woods and large Oaks—The House is a very Grand one much like Bessborough but its chief Beauty is its two Superb Staircases and Noble Gallery—It is altogether a very grand and venerable place and I felt a pleasure in hearing my mother [Martha Cuffe, daughter of John, first Lord Desart], recount the Many Happy Hours she spent in the large Hall where, in my Grandfathers time the family met and dined around a blazing Woodfire after the Manner of Old Times.*[2]

This is the stately Desart family and home that stuck in Hoban's mind to the zenith of his career. Similarities are readily observed in the White House frontage, the Palladian style of the bay frontage, Ionic columns, and entablature, and in the roofline. If tourists often comment that the White House appears smaller than expected, it is similar in height at least to Desart Court: two stories over a basement, with two two-story wings, to appear as a seat of power for a family of state.

A SEAT OF POWER

Of course Irish country houses were not simply summer vacation destinations, places for family weekends of hill-walking. These grand Irish houses were initially the base of year-round, serious, estate-wide enterprises. Country estates included a variety of farms, forests, schools, churches, families, servants, budding industries, communities, and countless responsibilities. Landowners such as Desart kept an active and heavy schedule related to tenant matters, relationships with farmers, crops, forestry, or livestock, and they managed these even from their city accommodations.

A key variant apart from the grand house in the city, however, was that much of the owner's business life in the Irish countryside involved outdoor sport, expansive pathways and gardens, and countryside pursuits. For important guests and business relations, the country house was meant to speak for its owner. Through libraries, bedrooms, ballrooms, and large, manicured gardens, the goal was to leave guests in no doubt of the owners' lifestyle and power within and over the land.

Leinster House, another influence on young Hoban, was originally designed by the German architect, Richard Castle, in 1745–50 near Dublin to be a ducal palace for the Earl of Kildare. While it has been said that it "is by no means the greatest Irish country house, its architecture a little stiff, its principal facade a bit squat,"[3] Leinster House—as it has been called since 1766, when the Earl of Kildare was created Duke of Leinster—became a cornerstone of influence in Hoban's designs of the White House for George Washington.

Leinster House had one of the first floor plans in Ireland to show a library for the ground floor. Libraries, or book rooms, did not consistently emerge in the floor plans of Irish country houses until the 1700s, when they were used to mark the status and reflect the education of their learned owner. The Earl of Kildare kept a large chest "for Bookes" in the study of his Dublin house in 1656.[4] Carton, the country house of Lord and Lady Kildare, had two libraries, one large and one small.

While a student, Hoban must have visited the building site of Leinster House frequently during its progressive remodels by the English architect James Wyatt. Wyatt's version of Leinster House can be seen in heavy influence on several seats of power: in Hoban's Charleston County Courthouse in South Carolina, which is also reflected in Hoban's first drawings for the White House; in Castletown House, home of William Conolly (1662–1729), Speaker of the Irish House of Commons, another seat of Irish power; in the White House ballroom, known as the East Room, largely based on the ballroom of Leinster House, which was built to fill the entire depth of the house from front to back at the northern end of the building; and in its current purpose as the seat of the Oireachtas Éireann, the Parliament of Ireland, following the Anglo-Irish Treaty of 1921.

A FAMILY HOME

Prominent Irish country houses were designed to bring stately city life to the country. Whether family life followed suit was a different matter. While the business carried on, Irish country houses were simultaneously family homes. They were retreats for the owners and their loved ones, away from the publicity and glare of city, a place where families could enjoy a relative privacy. Leinster House was initially designed to be a bit "out of the way" as a house for the Earl of Kildare to escape from the eyes and ears that followed him along the city streets, relatively speaking.[5] Staff and servants occupied the family spaces as well as the main rooms in which business was conducted. Here the real world of child rearing, gossip, family affairs, and laughter carried on.

British influence was infused into the architecture of Irish country houses, but life itself adapted to fit the family lifestyles of the Irish people. The marvelous trade for which the Irish are renowned—hospitality—set the Irish country home apart and meant that country living could be enjoyed by all sorts of guests in a relatively relaxed air. More rooms, more servants, and larger furniture were made to accommodate friends, and updates were made to original architectural designs in the eighteenth- and nineteenth-century heyday.

Bedrooms, suites, and closets were arranged to fit a domestic life structured between classes and stations. House plans varied in Irish country houses; however, they tended to include a bedroom on the ground floor up to the mid-eighteenth century, with the rest of the bedrooms upstairs in various configurations to support nurses, and dressing rooms and anterooms. The plans at Carton, where Lord and Lady Kildare lived in addition to Leinster House, showed these bedrooms opposite each other, so that the lord and ladyship could each retreat in the country privately or together as they wished.

The casual nature of the countryside in turn infused architecture. Libraries became more than places for reading. These spaces would eventually be filled with displays, curiosities, music, fine furniture, and parties. Libraries were frequently used as gathering spaces and rooms for the family as well as for entertainment. Windows of libraries began to be bowed in architectural designs to emit more of the soft countryside light throughout the day. A billiard room was placed adjacent to the library, where the racketing of balls and whiskey glasses could be heard after a long day's shoot or men could gather by the fire.

Over time, Irish country houses changed along with the life lived within them. The initial design of Leinster House was altered significantly over the half century that the family lived there. Some of these changes were carried out by the British architect James Wyatt, who was connected and likely closely collaborated with Lady Kildare, Emily Lennox, the fashionable daughter of the second Duke of Richmond who had a great passion for decoration and architecture. The Duke of Leinster's first son, William, was "kind and popular" and occupied the house while Hoban was a student in Dublin.[6] Later the Kildare family moved to their other beloved country house, Carton, also designed by the architect Richard Castle. After Leinster House was sold to the Dublin Society (later the Royal Dublin Society) in the early 1800s, its rooms were further adapted.

It was Hoban who convinced George Washington, a man with a passion for the countryside, of the attractiveness of the grand Irish country house as a model for the United States. One can easily understand why the design appealed to President Washington as a stately "Home for the Nation," as the White House is often affectionately called. Indeed, at the time of the White House's construction, the surrounding Potomac landscape, with its river, fields, and trees, appeared much like an Irish countryside estate of Hoban's youth.

There is perhaps no more iconic photograph than that of John F. Kennedy Jr. playing underneath his father's presidential desk in the Oval Office to illustrate the dual purpose that the White House has served as both a seat of power and a family home. It does not take a mental leap too far to envision the same image in a grand seventeenth-century house of the Irish countryside. Just as Lady Kildare did, First Lady Jacqueline Kennedy and other first ladies of the White House have adapted the White House's interior—both upper and lower floors—to fit each successive presidential family. These first ladies have applied unwavering charisma and substantial amounts of time to restoring portions of the White House for the country, for their children, and for posterity. The preservation of this historic house by supporters of the White House Historical Association remains a worthy responsibility.

ANGLO-IRISH RELATIONS

It is impossible to discuss the shape of Irish country houses or the life within them in recent centuries without also addressing the relationship of Great Britain and the Republic of Ireland. Much of the growth in housing followed the Acts of Union in 1800. Conflict still raged in the colors of flags across the political landscape, sometimes very painfully, but this period did experience increased travel and influence between the islands and the Continent. This allowed for eighteenth- and nineteenth-century European influences to infuse homes and discussions with a broader diversity of ideas. Many landowners increased rents over their tenants, funds that they used to build extensions and new frontages to old houses or to demolish old houses and build country houses anew.

The Great Famine of the 1840s diminished the pace of housing developments across Ireland. The Landlord and Tenant (Ireland) Act 1870, publication of *The Great Landowners of Great Britain and Ireland* (first published as *The Acre-Ocracy of England* in 1876), combined with outbreaks of agrarian unrest in Ireland in the latter part of the nineteenth-century, meant that many Anglo-Irish or British families moved back to London, and, in the process, many stately homes began to fall gradually into disrepair. After the Countess of Desart had left Desart Court, the fifth Earl of Desart and his family took up residence in 1899 and spent the next twenty years restoring the neglected house and grounds. As soon as 1903, he sold most of the surrounding land to his tenants, retaining just the house and gardens.

In 1922, Desart Court was burned to the ground in an attack by Irish Republicans directed at several estates in the countryside. At that time, Desart Court had stood for nearly two hundred years before an order from the high command of the antitreaty faction during the Irish Civil War demanded the burning of all houses occupied by senators of the governing Irish Free State. Desart Court was rebuilt for a time, before finally being demolished once again in the 1950s.

The absence of Desart Court and, indeed, portions of the original White House of the United States remind us that violence does not actually answer political questions and that people can rebuild. British soldiers torched much the original White House in the summer of 1814 during the War of 1812. Fortunately, the full-length painting of George Washington was famously saved from the flames by First Lady Dolley Madison and the White House was "repaired" for the country by Hoban, who used even the smallest of its remaining stones once again.

Acts of destruction have never succeeded in preventing Great Britain, Ireland, and the United States from becoming the closest of global allies. Indeed, the annual presentation of a lucky countryside flower, the shamrock, by an *taoiseach* (prime minister of Ireland) to the president of the United States takes place in the White House, modeled on Leinster House, designed by Irish architect, influenced by British architectural designs. This annual presentation is an act of poignant friendship. Like an architect's drawings, designs that honor the past but are not bound by it can lead to new and beautiful places upon the shared foundations of our history.

CONCLUSION

Country life and, in turn, country houses have changed dramatically since James Hoban's time. Since 1900, a significant percentage of undeveloped farmland across the island of Ireland has diminished. Large landownership has been reduced in much of Europe, as great estates have steadily become a fraction of their size, turned into summer houses or resorts, or as holdings have been broken up over successive generations, sold piecemeal, or new legislation is adopted. Of Carton, Leinster, Desart, Rockingham, Powerscourt, Lough Glynn, and Portumna, some are today's leading visitor attractions; some are houses of government; some are golf courses or wedding venues; and some no longer stand.

Yet echoes of the eighteenth and nineteenth centuries can still be felt through these well-built, stoic edifices of stone. In daily photographs on the nightly news, the influence of Leinster and Desart and their architects are visible in the White House and across the world. Lafayette Park, itself resembling a grand garden and forecourt, reminds us of the vast fields that surrounded and supported the eighteenth-century Irish country estates and on which toiled masses of farmers. The White House East Room and parlors allow the U.S. president to entertain, just as estate owners did in the ballrooms and parlors of the countryside centuries ago. The gardens of the White House host gatherings, concerts, and a holiday tree and menorah, and each spring children romp across the lawns as they participate in the White House Easter Egg Roll.

Life in cities shaped Irish country houses in the eighteenth century, while family life in the Irish countryside shaped those houses in return. Vital conversations between history and modernity, cosmopolitan and countryside, tradition and innovation, preservation and renewal remain close to home, important, and quotidian on the island of Ireland. I remain hopeful that the work of future generations in architecture and in other fields will, like Hoban's, aspire to provide us with beautiful spaces in libraries, ballrooms, quite corners, forums, and open gardens where people can continue to gather in peace. Just as architecture has the ability to inspire, country life leaves us simultaneously replenished, mindful of our duty of care, aware of our surrounding communities, conscious of the bounty and importance of our farmlands, and with a sense of shared belonging in the natural world. The country house will long be a place we call home, a place for us to return.

NOTES

1. *Retrospections of Dorothea Herbert*, vol. 1, *1770–1789* (London: Gerhard Howe, 1929) quoted in "Desart Court, Talbotsinch," www.kierankilkenny.wixsite.com.
2. Ibid.
3. Text by William Seale in Bruce White, "Four Places in Hoban's Dublin: A Twenty-First Century Photographer's View," *White House History*, no. 22 (Spring 2008): 70.
4. Patricia McCarthy, *Life in the County House in Georgian Ireland* (New Haven: Paul Mellon Centre for Studies in British Art, 2016).
5. Seale in White, "Four Places in Hoban's Dublin," 70.
6. Ibid.

V. BRIAN O'CONNELL

James Hoban and George Washington Devise the President's House

John F. Kennedy, the first serving president of the United States to visit Ireland, addressed the Oireachtas, the Irish Parliament, at its seat in Leinster House, Dublin, on June 28, 1963:

> *It has also been said by some that a few of the features of this stately mansion served to inspire similar features in the White House in Washington. Whether this is true or not, I know that the White House was designed by James Hoban, a noted Irish-American architect and I have no doubt that he believed by incorporating several features of the Dublin style he would make it more homelike for any president of Irish descent. It was a long wait, but I appreciate his efforts.*[1]

How did it come about that James Hoban, with the tripartite distinction of being Catholic, a peasant, and an Irishman, all potentially anathema to the establishment of the time, designed and built the house that remains today as an icon or symbolic expression of the United States?

Hoban designed what is essentially a neo-Palladian house, based on certain received northern European canons in the language of architecture. President George Washington informed its design. He was known to admire the Duke of Leinster's public-spirited family[2] and to have regarded the house of this "First Gentleman" of Ireland as the architectural ideal for the first magistrate of the new American republic: enough state, but not too much. The public seems to have agreed. N. P. Willis, an early commentator, observed, "The residence of the Chief Magistrate of the United States resembles the country seat of an English nobleman, in its architecture and size.... It is a commodious and creditable building, serving its purpose without too much state for a republican country."[3]

PALLADIO'S CANONS

"Neo-Palladianism" is the name given to the early and mid-eighteenth-century application of the books of Andrea Palladio. The Palladian Canons of Architecture were progressively elaborated into more refined design applications in subsequent well-tempered pattern book designs.[4] Palladio, like other Renaissance authors on the subject, believed that architecture derived from an awareness of the instinct to order the shaping of the national environment to corporate human and social purpose. The

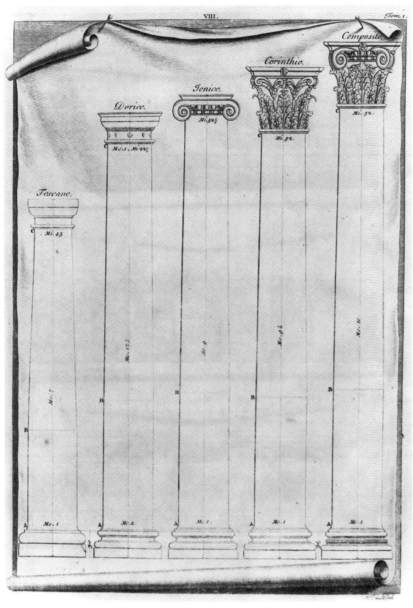

Andrea Palladio's five orders of classical design were based on column design, three Greek (Doric, Ionic, Corinthian) and two Roman (Tuscan, Composite), and they were believed to be essentially related to the human scale and form. Palladio featured this illustration of the columns in his book, I Quattro Libri dell'Architettura *(1570).*

reverence for antiquity was grounded in the eighteenth-century cultural assumption that Greece and Rome had reached perfection in all of the arts, including architecture. Apart from surviving buildings and ruins, an ancient text from the beginning of the Christian era by Vitruvius, entitled *De Architectura*, without illustration, was the only known literary basis for understanding the principles of classical architecture. With the advent of printing, the Vitruvius text, with derivative illustrative drawings annexed, led to the publication of a series of Renaissance texts, like Palladio's, that presented the classical canons of architectural design with new illustrations and ingenious applications. The five orders, any one of which fixed the character of a use, were based on column design, three Greek (Doric, Ionic, Corinthian) and two Roman (Tuscan, Composite), all of which were believed to be essentially related to the human scale and form.

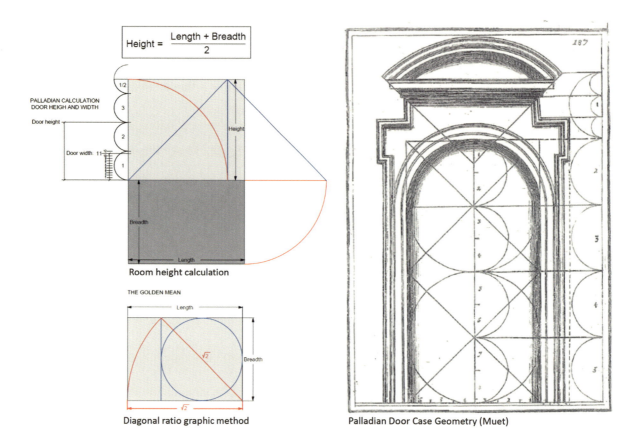

The author's analysis of door case geometry (as illustrated by Palladio on the right) highlights the square and the circle as the generators of all derivative rules. Palladio suggested that in the absence of any standard of measurement, a single element—in this case, a door case—divided into squares and circles, could be set as the module from which all other related dimensions could be derived in an enclosed system.

    Palladio, in the spirit of the Renaissance, advanced canons for architectural design on the basis of both reason and experience. The canons were grounded in geometry and proportion. The square and the circle were the generators of all derivative rules. Squares, subdivisions of squares, or rational increments of lines, squares, and circles, or their combinations, were at the base of all Palladian canons. The division of squares and circles into rational parts was an essential. In the absence of any standard of measurement, a single element—customarily the diameter of the base of a column—was set as a module from which all other related dimensions were derived in an enclosed system. The essence of this internal system of proportion was symmetry, or the relationship of each part to the whole.

    Inigo Jones brought Palladio's canons to England in the early seventeenth century, and in the early eighteenth century Edward Lovett Pearce brought Palladianism to Ireland, where it informed the development of civic and domestic architecture and came to be readily understood by ordinary people. At the Dublin Society School of Architectural Drawing, Hoban was educated in neo-Palladianism, and he consolidated his understanding of it through his experience of public buildings in Ireland. For the new seat of government on the Potomac, Hoban's neo-Palladianism exactly suited Washington's architectural aspirations.

HOBAN'S DESIGNS

The geometry of Palladio was the basis of both architecture and building practice in the last decades of the eighteenth century. In Dublin, Hoban learned drawing together with geometry as an architectural discipline and basis for design. The process was laborious, with instruments that were primitive by modern standards. Paper was coarse and unstable; scales were boxwood or ivory as the most stable materials available; pens used capillary nibs; and the T-square, set square, compass, and dividers were the basic instruments by which the geometric forms that grounded design were represented.

Before the advent of standard units of measurement or reliable tape measures, the compass was the most diverse and flexible of the available instruments, easily replicated on site in setting out work using a cord with a fixed peg in the ground at one end and a swinging marker peg at the other to set out a point, or curve. Palladian geometric forms were all easily and accurately attained by this simple instrument. For example, the golden mean—the ratio between the side and diagonal of a square—was found accurately on paper or on the ground by swinging the arc of the compass from the diagonal to extend one side of a square; likewise a square was assured by equating the diagonals by use of the compass.

Palladian ratios directed Hoban's designs for the President's House, in plan, elevation, and section. The geometric layout of his competition plan and its corresponding adjusted proposal can be shown on analysis to demonstrate that the Palladian geometric canons of design are their generator. It can be said that the whole of the plan is based on the Ionic column module and that the plan divisions that are shown to be, within that module, based on a composition of squares, extended to the diagonal ratio where circumstances require it. The elevation is likewise regulated by the same modular discipline, where intercolumniation by reference to the module follows a disciplined pattern.

As a final reference to the Palladian canon, I have carried out a study of both the windows and the entablature as designed by Hoban as subelements within the design that demonstrate the application of the canonical geometric control to ensure the symmetry of the parts in the design as a whole. This study demonstrates the use of a combination of squares, circles, and extended diagonals. The window hoods are regulated by the height of the window opening.

Training in architectural drawing made the geometric forms used in building intuitive to the architects and builders like Hoban and formed a part of the language of architectural propriety, referable to Palladian rules, which as a prevailing classical imagery was familiar also to Washington; he speaks of it in his correspondence. While the President's House was a competent and authentic neo-Palladian design in the context of its time, it did not reflect the then avant-garde fashion of neo-classicism. For that very reason, it spoke to the character of George Washington, the president who desired that the President's House should express stability and order as the symbolic home of the new nation at a time of great political and social uncertainty.

50

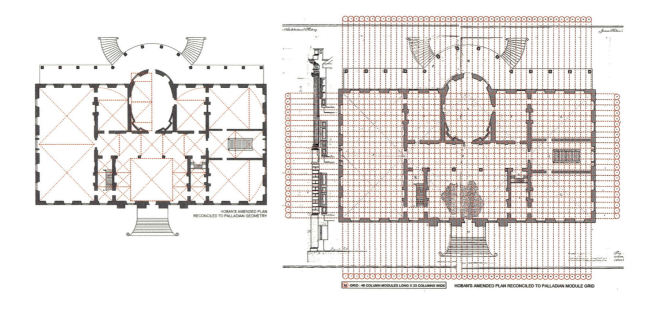

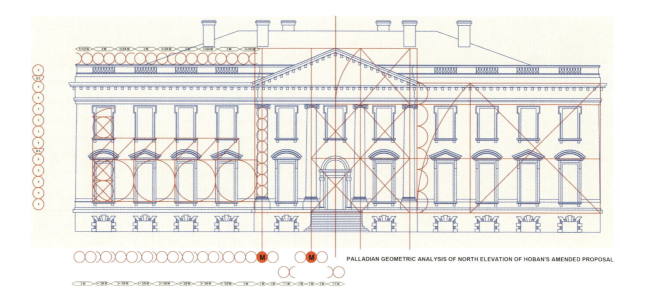

Palladian ratios directed Hoban's designs for the President's House in plan, elevation, and section. His floor plan (top) and north elevation (bottom) can be analyzed with a Palladian module grid to demonstrate their basis in Palladian geometric canons of design. Hoban's plan is based on the Ionic column module, and the plan divisions are based on a composition of squares, extended by the same modular discipline, where the module follows a disciplined pattern.

HOBAN AND WASHINGTON

In a letter of July 30, 1792, Washington wrote to his secretary Tobias Lear:

> *I found at George town many well conceived, & ingenious plans for Public buildings in the New City: it was a pleasure indeed, to find—in an infant country—such a display of Architectural abilities. The Plan of Mr. Hoben who was introduced to me by Doctr Tucker, from Charleston, & who appears to be a very judicious man, was made choice of for the President's House, and the Commissioners have agreed with him to superintend the building of it—& that of the Capitol also, if they should, hereafter, be disposed to put both under one management. He has been engaged in some of the first buildings in Dublin—appears a master workman—and has a great many hands of his own. He has laid out the foundation which is now digging & will be back in a month to enter heartily upon the work.*[5]

The subtext of this letter demonstrates the confidence of Washington in Hoban. It is evident that their temperaments have engaged as complementary. Hoban is acknowledged as a "master of workmen." He is seen as an energetic and "very judicious man," capable of judgment and so to be trusted. The use of the terms "master workman" and "Architectural abilities" coalesce to establish the ideal amanuensis. Washington's instinct in the circumstances of an "infant country" were right: his was to be a real partnership with Hoban for the remainder of Washington's life.

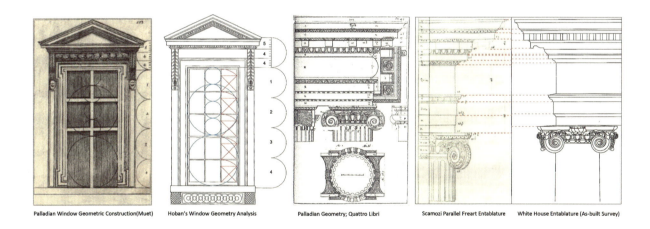

Studying both the windows and the entablature as designed by Hoban (second and fifth from left) against Palladio's own window and entablatures (first and third from the left) demonstrates the application of the canonical geometric control to ensure the symmetry of the parts in the design as a whole. This analysis highlights Hoban's use of a combination of squares, circles, and the diagonal ratio. White House column capitals, in Hoban's final iteration, deviate from the Palladian model as shown above, and follow Scamozzi's diagonal variant. This variant addresses the bidirectional symmetry of corner columns and was the form favored by Inigo Jones and carried over into the Irish Palladian tradition.

Hoban's initial design was approved: it was a substantial neo-Palladian house following the pattern established in Dublin by Richard Castle, particularly in Leinster House, now the seat of the Irish Oireachtas or Parliament, and in the Lying-In Hospital. The remaining evidence of Hoban's original proposal, as derived from the north wall section adjoining the surviving plan, shows that the original submission was based on a partly rusticated podium floor, a fully fenestrated *piano nobile*, and an attic story; the roof was pitched and terminating to a stone balustrade. A projecting entrance front in the giant tetrastyle Ionic order was engaged on the entrance axis to the north, which axis was projected southward through to the garden front as the long axis to a central elliptical room on the north-south axis and south bow with loggia terrace to the south. The whole composition appears to have been set to a basement to the north and a podium floor to the garden elevation to the south. No pediment is shown to the north front in the section. While possibly none was intended, it seems probable, having regard to the Hoban-amended north elevation, to prevailing practice, and to the probable reference buildings, that a pediment was included in the original submission of 1792 and merely not picked up on the surviving section.

The record shows that the design was developed from the competition submission by Hoban in consultation with Washington. Due to limitation on stone available and cost, Washington agreed to omit the ground floor, including the rusticated entrance, bringing the *piano nobile* to plinth level to the north while remaining a single level above the gardens to the south. The record is instructive in illuminating the relationship between Washington and Hoban. Concerning the phasing of the larger building, the president wrote to the Commissioners for the District of Columbia, "It was my idea (and, if I am not mistaken, Mr. Hoben coincided with the propriety and practically of it) that the building be so arranged that only a part of it should be erected at present; but upon such a plan as to make the part so erected an entire building, and to admit of an addition in the future."[6]

Here is clearly the relationship of gentleman patron and architect amanuensis, one conceiving an aspect of the idea, the other expressing it and confirming it as both appropriate and that it can be achieved in architectural terms as practical. The relationship between Washington and Hoban, in which mutual understanding led to accommodation, explains the continuous success of Hoban with the president, where others failed. The required outcome at every level lay in Hoban's willingness and ability by competence and temperament to secure Washington's vision—that is, in a more subtle meaning, to act as a true amanuensis to lead and serve at the same time.

Hoban was born to the traditions of the Irish peasantry, an ancient, dignified, self-sufficient but defeated people who were marked by Catholicism as the natural foil to their spirit and who through political necessity learned to survive in an unequal society by developing a metaphysical character, in which one could adjust reality to advantage through imaginative perception, humor, and skilled manipulation of influences. In engagement with those who asserted superiority or were themselves vulnerable to criticism, the Irish peasantry had an ability to manage language inventively, developing through this a cultural response that was to characterize them to the rest of the world for better or worse. Hoban's peasant status endowed him with the temperament necessary to succeed in an emerging society where reward was based on competence.

Even before he learned architectural drawing, Hoban was trained as a carpenter and wheelwright on the Desart Court estate where he grew up. A carpenter in the last quarter of the eighteenth century was a more responsible position in construction than it later was. Because of the important part played

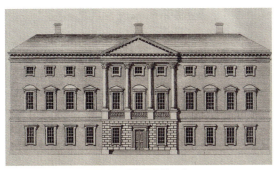

LEINSTER HOUSE Oireachtas
By Cassells- Pool and Cash (1779)

LYING-IN HOSPITAL Rotunda
By Cassells- Pool and Cash (1779)

A tentative reconstruction by the author of Hoban's lost original design for the President's House, based on the surviving records (bottom), reveals a substantial neo-Palladian house following the pattern established in Dublin by Richard Castle. Hoban's reference to Dublin buildings is seen particularly in Leinster House and in the Lying-In Hospital (top). This first design was based on a partly rusticated podium floor, a fully fenestrated first floor, and an attic story with a pitched roof terminating to a stone balustrade. A projecting entrance front in the giant tetrastyle Ionic order was placed on the entrance axis to the north. While a pediment was possibly not intended, it seems probable that it was when considering Hoban's amended north elevation, prevailing practice, and the probable reference buildings.

by timber in the masonry structures, the carpenter regulated the activities of other artisans employed at building sites. The carpenter also installed windows, hung doors, provided wooden partitions and framework supports for decorative plaster, and designed and built roofs.[7] Francis Price's *British Carpenter* (1753) insists, "As all building are composed of three principal parts, viz, strength, use and beauty, therefore carpentry naturally comes in among the essential heads of Architecture."[8] At the School of Architectural Drawing, Hoban advanced his occupation. His knowledge of architecture was not an academic pursuit. He was a "practical architect."

Washington was by temperament a gentleman of his time and place. His father had favored his elder brothers, sending them to England to be educated. With a limited local education, Washington created an admirable alternative character for himself and regulated it through iron discipline the rest of his life. He practiced discretion as an art. He set objectives and secured them through careful and meticulous application based on a pragmatic intelligence, tempered by a diplomatic charm. He was impatient of criticism, possibly an unmasterable insecurity from childhood. Notwithstanding a limited classical education by comparison with those around him, he clearly aspired to a knowledge and understanding of architecture as an extension of some knowledge of classical languages, classical history, and art. These were the attributes of a gentleman within the social matrix of his youth and middle years.[9]

Following the success of the Revolution, Washington set as his objective the founding of the new nation. Once the decision was made to move the seat of government from Philadelphia to a new federal capital that would express the spirit of the nation, it became Washington's priority to procure the required buildings for the city that was now planned. Not unreasonably, he accepted the neo-Palladian norms of his early and middle years as the appropriate form of architectural and urban expression. It seems clear that his temperament was not to be overawed by new fashions or advancing orders of taste. He had taught himself to be pragmatic in his confidence: he knew what he wanted and would get it. Hoban, the practical architect, a diligent perceptive Irishman now secure in society yet bred with an innate peasant's deference to the gentry, was the perfect partner in achieving the ambition of his patron.

By reference to the outcome, Washington's choice was right on all counts. A "typical gentleman's country house," as illustrated in James Gibbs's *Book of Architecture* (1728), was Washington's expectation in terms of architectural dignity and appropriate form, "without too much state for a republican country." This was also the architectural intuition to which Hoban was bred. Leinster House as a model in the same idiom, familiar to Hoban, would bring the associations Washington sought of the equivalent to the residence of the first magistrate of the Kingdom of Ireland, itself on the cusp of a similar revolution.

In his later years, it was Washington's life's mission to succeed in consolidating the federation that was the United States and to express a federal capital that would stand as a symbolic bulwark against the possible reluctance of the member states to submit to federal control. With Hoban, the practical architect, as his temperamental complement, Washington achieved not only visible success in the building of the President's House and new capital in Washington City, but also history's judgment that the hero of the Revolution and the Father of His Country was the only one who could have secured the unity of the new nation as well.

The White House survives today as a symbol of the United States of America, the home of its first citizen and magistrate, a backdrop to the actions of the Executive. Beyond Palladian geometry, the forces that determined it were the compatibility and a tacit partnership between the minds of Hoban and Washington. The White House is American, but of European origin and of Irish descent. Deep within its permanent aura it holds the united temperaments and talents of the first gentleman and the practical architect, conserving a unique and enduring expression of the United States of America.

And thus through this tacit constructive partnership between George Washington and James Hoban, the White House was first devised.

NOTES

This essay is an abbreviated version of the author's presentation at the White House Historical Association symposium "The United Kingdom and Ireland in the White House: A Conversation on Historical Perspectives," Washington, D.C., April 17, 2018.

1. John F. Kennedy, "Address Before the Irish Parliament," June 28, 1963, available on the John F. Kennedy Library and Museum website, jfklibrary.org.
2. William Seale, *The White House: The History of an American Idea*, 2nd ed. (Washington, D.C.: White House Historical Association, 2001), 6.
3. N. P. Willis, *American Scenery; or, Land, Lake, and River Illustrations of Transatlantic Nature* (London: Virtue, 1840), 2:32.
4. Andrea Palladio's *Four Books of Architecture* were published in Venice in 1570 and in London, in a full English edition, in 1715, which was among the standard text in the Dublin Society School of Architectural Drawing in Hoban's time.
5. George Washington to Tobias Lear, July 30, 1792, in *Letters and Recollections of George Washington, Being Letters to Tobias Lear and Others Between 1790 and 1799* (New York: Doubleday, Page, 1906), 57–58, available on *Founders Online* website, founders.archives/gov.
6. George Washington to Commissioners for the District of Columbia, March 3, 1793, George Washington Papers, Library of Congress, Washington, D.C., reprinted in *The Writings of George Washington Relating to the National Capital*, published in *Records of the Columbia Historical Society* 17 (1914): 76–77.
7. Arthur Gibney, *The Building Site in Eighteenth-Century Ireland* (Dublin: Four Courts Press, 2017), 57.
8. Francis Price, *The British Carpenter; or, A Treatise on Carpentry* (London: printed by C. and J. Ackers for C. Hitch and L. Hawes, 1753), introduction [n.p.]
9. For modern analyses of Washington's character, see John Ferling, *The Ascent of George Washington: The Hidden Political Genius of an American Icon* (New York: Bloomsbury Press, 2009); Richard Norton Smith, *Patriarch: George Washington and the New American Nation* (Boston: Houghton Mifflin, 1993); Richard Brookhiser, *Founding Father: Rediscovering George Washington* (New York: Free Press, 1996); Alan Taylor, *American Revolutions: A Continental History, 1750–1804* (New York: W. W. Norton, 2016), 396.

VI. ANDREW McCARTHY

James Hoban's 1792 Designs for the President's House

James Hoban's winning entry in the 1792 design competition for the President's House is today almost lost to history. Only one page of drawings survives, preserved in the collection of the Massachusetts Historical Society. With enough research into Hoban's background and architectural experience, and some informed guesswork to supplement gaps in the surviving record, the essence of his original plan for the President's House takes shape.

JAMES HOBAN'S PLAN

Hoban's surviving plan shows the ground floor of the house, essentially as built. But a diagram on the left side of the page confirms that the house originally had three stories, not two, above a raised basement. The north front was to feature a rusticated centerpiece at entry level. Additionally, the first floor plan shows a long colonnaded porch or gallery, likely one story tall, spanning the whole south front. Surviving letters reveal that the footprint of Hoban's initial design was subsequently enlarged by one-fifth, at George Washington's request. Afterward, to save money, Hoban removed one floor from his first proposal, resulting in the two-story, 168-foot-long house we know.[1]

Since the rediscovery and publication of Hoban's competition drawings in 1916 by the art historian Fiske Kimball, scholars have disagreed about how to interpret them. While William Ryan and Desmond Guinness argue that Hoban's 1792 design included a pediment on the North Front, William Seale, in his larger overall history of the White House, notes that Hoban's wall diagram shows a simple balustraded parapet.[2] Clearly, studying today's White House in isolation is not enough to reconstruct properly Hoban's first proposal for the President's House.

To do so requires consideration both of James Hoban's background as an Irish immigrant and of his practice as an architect. Although few of Hoban's architectural papers still exist, some survive via secondhand copies. Such is the case with Charles Bulfinch's tracings of Hoban's original drawings for the current North Portico of the White House.

Bulfinch's copies reveal that Hoban considered two different intercolumniations for the sides of the portico. The setup now in place is decidedly unorthodox, featuring a distinctive pair of columns in the middle. However, Hoban's unused diagram features a much more typical arrangement of individual columns. This reveals that Hoban's North Portico—often criticized for its unusual character—was not the result of architectural ineptitude but rather a deliberate design choice. Not only that, Hoban provided a more conventional alternative, which was rejected.[3]

If Hoban followed similar practice in 1792, it is possible that he submitted alternative designs for the North Facade of the President's House—one version with a pediment and another without.[4] That question aside, what did his initial facade look like? Was it as stylistically conservative as the current White House, with its Anglo-Palladian detailing? Or, like the later North Portico, did it follow a different pattern? After all, Hoban was highly recommended to President Washington by the citizens of his adopted hometown, Charleston, South Carolina. Why would men like Henry Laurens so esteem Hoban's architectural talents if he had little new to offer his clients?[5]

The answer undoubtedly lies buried in Hoban's own Irish background. It has long been a commonplace of White House scholarship that Hoban's basic design was modeled on Leinster House, the grandest town house in eighteenth-century Dublin.[6] But, as Seale suggests, the balustraded North Front of his 1792 design surely comes from Desart Court, the country house in County Kilkenny on whose demesne Hoban was born. Moreover, by Hoban's own account, he helped build the great masterpiece of 1780s Irish neoclassicism, James Gandon's Dublin Custom House.[7]

Details linked to these buildings reappear, in surprising ways, in American works associated with Hoban. A surviving sketch of the White House North Front by Samuel Blodgett (for whom Hoban designed Blodgett's Hotel in Washington, D.C.) shows the house largely as built—except with a pair of crossed laurel branches in the central frieze.[8] This motif strongly echoes a crossed fasces and liberty pole that adorn the facade of James Gandon's Nottingham County Hall.[9]

Samuel Blodgett is commonly credited with designing the First Bank of the United States in Philadelphia. Nonetheless, historians agree that the model for the bank's facade was the Dublin Royal Exchange, prompting some to suggest Hoban was somehow involved in its design.[10] But while the exchange interior is dominated by a rotunda, the Philadelphia bank originally featured a barrel-vaulted teller room that strongly echoed the vaulted and colonnaded Long Room, the commercial nexus of Gandon's Dublin Custom House.[11] The bank's facade also innovated, by adding an inscription with the date of construction—a motif shared by the principal front of Desart Court.[12] The confluence of these Irish models may suggest the hidden hand of Hoban at work.

From these details we can begin to build a larger portrait of Hoban the architect. Like any good draftsman, he drew inspiration for his buildings from multiple sources at once. These models appear to have been principally (if not exclusively) ones he had encountered as a young man in Ireland. He was also clearly attracted to the work of James Gandon, the most fashionable architect of late eighteenth-century Ireland. In the view of Irish architectural historian Edward McParland, Gandon's design style was quite deliberately manneristic, bending the rules of architecture in a playful spirit.[13] The surviving alternative designs for Hoban's North Portico reveal this same mannerist tendency at work.

Nor were all of Hoban's models drawn from real-life observation. Given the immense popularity of pattern books among eighteenth-century architects, Hoban undoubtedly drew on books and treatises as well as on physical edifices. Among his literary sources was certainly Robert Adam's book of engravings of the ruins of the Roman emperor Diocletian's palace in Split, Croatia.[14] From Adam's drawings, Hoban derived the distinctive arched design of the Palladian windows on the President's House—another highly unusual architectural feature.

In reconstructing Hoban's 1792 competition design, therefore, attention must be paid to features that orthodox architects might dismiss as nonstandard. Analysis of the surviving wall diagram throws up one such detail immediately: the height of the Ionic columns is apparently too great. In fact, Hoban reckoned the columns' standard height (nine diameters) not according to their total extent, as in normal practice, but rather according to their shafts only, excluding bases and capitals.

Equally, Hoban's drawing indicates two string courses running between the first and second floors, as at Leinster House. Normally, in such cases, the bottom of the two courses is the taller. Hoban deliberately zigzagged this rule by making his upper course the taller one but then dividing it into two smaller parts. Such a detail indicates the work of a playful architect, one who knows the rules of design and yet is willing to bend them for the sake of novelty. In this respect, Hoban suddenly appears closer stylistically to James Gandon than to his more conservative Anglo-Palladian predecessors whose work appears so well encapsulated in today's White House.

THE BUILDING'S FABRIC

Having established the architectural theory underpinning Hoban's 1792 designs, we can now reconstruct the details of the building's fabric. The outlying portions of the North Facade, the subject of the surviving wall diagram, are relatively easy to envision. Likewise, given the fact that Hoban's initial design was approximately five-sixths the size of the current house, the overall scale is not difficult to determine. Assuming an intercolumniation or separation of four diameters for the northern Ionic columns, and a standard spacing of cornice modillions, it emerges that Hoban's house would have been 142 feet long and 71 feet deep (excluding the southern bow and veranda). These are almost exactly the dimensions of Leinster House.

The centerpiece of the North Facade and the details of the south and side fronts are more difficult to assess, but these, too, can be reconstructed via reference to Hoban's probable inspirations. These design sources can be ascertained by a close look at the details of Hoban's surviving North Front diagram.

Whereas the final White House has smooth-shafted Ionic columns and a plain entablature enlivened only by Corinthian-style dentils, Hoban's 1792 drawing shows stop-fluted columns, a richly carved orthodox Ionic entablature, and *paterae* (roundels) in the central North Front frieze. The outermost second-floor windows have flat heads, but those of the centerpiece are not visible. The first-floor rustication, meanwhile, has square-edged grooves between the stones instead of the beveled edges more commonly used.[15]

Hoban's use of squared rustication suggests that one of his sources was the first three books of *Vitruvius Britannicus*, whose author Colen Campbell frequently (and sometimes inaccurately) depicted such rustication in his plates of English buildings.[16] The combination of fluted columns and *paterae*, however, attests to the stylistic influence of the then-current leader among neoclassical architects, Robert Adam.

Adam's published design for 20 St. James's Square, London, was almost certainly a model for the northern centerpiece of Hoban's 1792 President's House. That building featured a three-bay rustic arcade at ground level, on which rested four fluted Corinthian pilasters, supporting a frieze adorned with *paterae* and a balustraded roof parapet. Adam's facade at 20 St. James's Square was published in his 1778 book of architectural designs–*The Works in Architecture of Robert and James Adam*[17]–and thus easily available for reference by architects like Hoban.

Like Adam, Hoban presumably used a first-story arcade to support his Ionic columns on the North Front. (Hoban's original front door probably had a wooden lintel supporting a fanlight, as at the Bank of the United States.) The central second-floor northern windows were virtually certain to have had some special treatment—probably pedimented window hoods, with balustraded pedestals beneath. This arrangement creates an overall motif of flat-headed second-floor outer windows flanking a three-bay centerpiece, with more elaborate windows between the central columns.

Such a design strongly resembles the Rotunda Hospital (Lying-In Hospital) in Dublin. This was designed by Richard Castle, the German-born Irish architect who also built Leinster House; in fact, Castle based the Hospital's facade on his early designs for Leinster House.[18] This similarity suggests that Hoban was keenly aware not only of his own project's inspirations but also of those buildings' architects and their oeuvres as a whole.

The sides of Hoban's 1792 house no doubt featured as a second-floor centerpiece the Palladian windows that exist in modified form on today's White House. Some differences are naturally to be expected, however. As in Adam's engravings of Diocletian's Palace, Hoban may at first have wanted his windows' modillion cornices (but not their unusually large architraves) to be enriched with carved detail.

Moreover, in place of the pulvinated frieze and polychrome column shafts of Diocletian's Palace, Hoban presumably used an arrangement of *paterae* in the frieze, along with fluted columns. Similar *paterae* adorn the second-story windows of 20 St. James's Square. In fact, *paterae* also appear on the White House's Palladian windows in William Strickland's detailed engraving of the burned-out house after the fire of 1814.[19] Because Hoban rebuilt these windows entirely after the fire, he may have altered that particular detail during the reconstruction.

The 1792 windows' fluted Ionic columns would have been exactly the height of the rods in the lower third of the North Front's stop-fluted Ionic columns—another manneristic detail. Brackets must have supported the window columns, and, between them, some sort of adornment, most likely a swag garland.

Below the Palladian window there was probably a rusticated tripartite window with a quoined Gibbs surround, echoing the first-story rustic centerpiece on the north side. Such rusticated windows are a prominent feature of the basement of the current White House, but they are conspicuously absent from the basement in Hoban's 1792 drawing.

The current South Front, with its one-story bowed porch, has proved hardest for previous scholars to reconstruct. Due to imperfections in Hoban's plan as drawn, the column diameters appear too small to support an architrave of stone. In fact, this is undoubtedly an error born of on-the-fly corrections made elsewhere in the floor plan.[20]

The columns of the south veranda were undoubtedly meant to be of stone and would have spanned the full height of the first floor, supporting an entablature between the first and second stories. While the first floor would feature a covered porch, the lead flats of the porch roof would presumably have formed an open-air terrace for the second floor. This flat roof would have been drained by downspouts hidden in the columns, a technique used by James Gandon at the Dublin Custom House.[21]

Analysis of Hoban's floor plan reveals that, while the central bow of the rear porch likely featured the Doric order, the porch flanks, which have irregular intercolumniations, were no doubt essentially Tuscan. This arrangement recalls the principal facade of Desart Court, where a Doric order spanned the three central bays of the first floor. The porch would have been screened by an iron railing between the columns. The railing's central bay would probably have featured an ornamental panel, perhaps incorporating the cipher US, a play on the Roman tradition of using the initials SPQR to indicate official government works. The iron railing on the front steps of the William Seabrook House, a plantation home on Edisto Island South Carolina, long attributed to James Hoban, likewise displays the owner's initials:

WS.²² The lone mask keystone that in this reconstruction adorns the rustic basement below the colonnaded porch is also a detail taken from Desart Court; it presumably represented Poseidon or the Potomac, just as the Dublin Custom House was adorned with keystones personifying Irish rivers.²³

Hoban's plan suggests a house set in level ground—a feature obviously inconsistent with the terrain of the actual site. In fact, as Seale has noted, Hoban stopped at the Federal City to "view the ground" before meeting with President Washington in Philadelphia.²⁴ He no doubt knew about the pronounced slope of the ground in question and would have planned accordingly. The level south steps at the top of the surviving drawing can probably be explained simply by Hoban's having run out of room at the top of the page.

RECONSTRUCTION OF JAMES HOBAN'S BASIC EXTERIOR DESIGN WITH NORTH FACADE VARIANTS

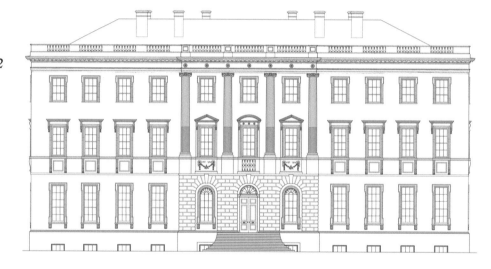

A reconstruction by the author of the North Front of James Hoban's 1792 President's House competition design. Here one can see the balustraded parapet that was originally meant to adorn the North Facade.

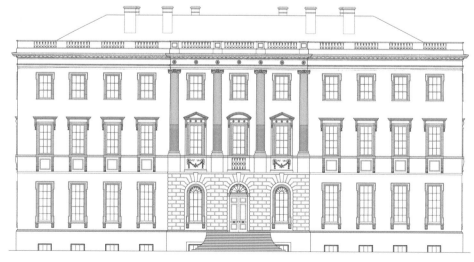

It is likely Hoban would have offered Washington the choice between minor exterior variants. In this drawing all three of the central second-floor windows have paterae *ornaments in their friezes, and the block rustication on the North Front is styled differently from that in the previous drawing.*

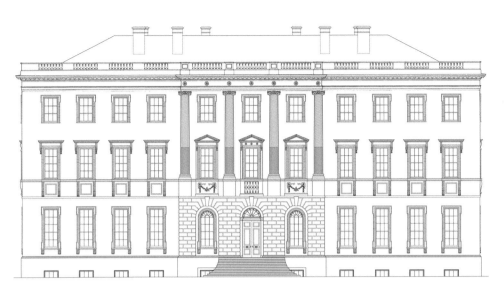

Another possible variant, seen here, would give the three central windows identical triangular pediments, instead of alternating triangular and segmental forms.

A reconstruction of the West Front of James Hoban's 1792 competition design. Note how the Palladian window is located on the second floor, above a tripartite window with a quoined Gibbs surround.

A reconstruction of James Hoban's 1792 South Front design. The one-story stone porch features a Doric order around the central bow, contrasting with Tuscan sections at left and right. The flat roof of the porch would have been drained by downspouts in the columns.

RECONSTRUCTION OF JAMES HOBAN'S EXTERIOR DESIGN WITH PEDIMENT IN THE STYLE OF ROBERT ADAM (WITH NORTH FACADE VARIANT)

The author's reconstructions of Hoban's design for the North Front (below and opposite) show that, like Adam, Hoban may have used a first-story arcade to support Ionic columns. The central second-floor northern windows were likely to have had a special treatment— such as pedimented window hoods, with balustraded pedestals beneath. These more elaborate windows, set between the central columns, would have been flanked by the flat-headed second-floor outer windows visible on Hoban's surviving wall diagram. The entrance hall would have had arched windows within the rustic centerpiece.

Design for 20 St. James's Square, London (right), by Robert Adam, showing Corinthian pilasters above a rusticated arcade.

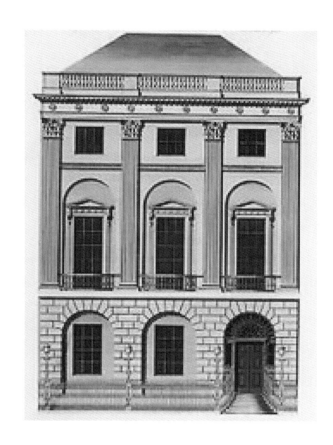

Reconstruction of the North Front of James Hoban's 1792 design, showing a pediment inspired by Robert Adam's buildings. Adam often used oversize roundels in pediments; the austere wreath-and-arrows carving seen here recurs in Charles Bulfinch's copies of Hoban's later drawings for the North Portico.

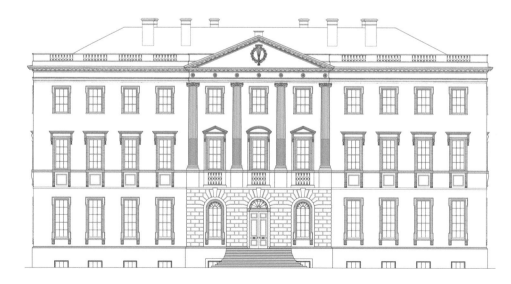

Another example of the many variations on external details that Hoban would have shown to Washington: the central second-floor window has a frieze adorned with fluting, modeled on the Dublin Royal Exchange exterior. The rustication seen here and in the prior drawing is patterned after the facade of 20 St. James's Square in London (opposite).

Reconstruction of the West Front of James Hoban's 1792 competition design, seen here with a pediment on the North Facade.

Another reconstruction drawing of James Hoban's 1792 South Front, showing an Adamesque variant on the Doric porch. The carved triglyphs above the outer flanking columns are modeled on those used in Robert Adam's entrance gateway to Syon House in London.

RECONSTRUCTION OF JAMES HOBAN'S EXTERIOR DESIGN WITH PEDIMENT IN THE STYLE OF JAMES GANDON (WITH NORTH FACADE VARIANT)

The Custom House in Dublin designed by James Gandon in 1781. James Hoban stated in his letter of introduction to the Commissioners for the District of Columbia that he was employed on the construction of this building.

A second pedimented reconstruction for the North Front of Hoban's 1792 competition design, this one based on the work of James Gandon. Here the carved wreath in the pediment is augmented in a more traditional fashion by a cluster of olive branches.

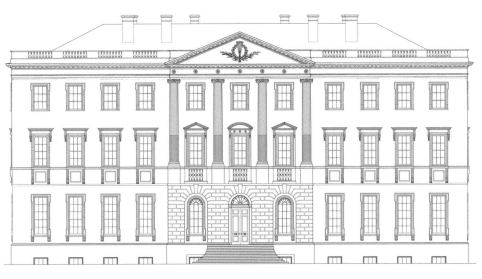

Variant of a "Gandonesque" North Front reconstruction for Hoban's 1792 competition design, featuring paterae *in the central window frieze. The rustication pattern on the ground floor is modeled on the garden front of Desart Court.*

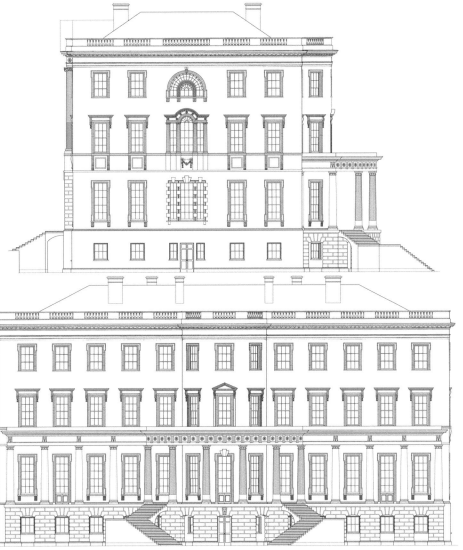

Gandonesque reconstruction of the West Front of James Hoban's 1792 competition design, with a pediment on the North Facade. The bucrania *(ox-skulls) over the Tuscan columns of the south porch are inspired by the frieze of Gandon's Custom House.*

Gandonesque reconstruction of James Hoban's 1792 South Front design. In this version the flutes on the central Doric columns of the porch stop at dado level, a detail that also appears in James Gandon's initial designs for the Dublin Custom House.

THE INTERIOR OF THE HOUSE

The interior of the house, and the probable purposes of its various rooms, can equally be reconstructed with a fair degree of certainty. It is well-known that Hoban's general model for the floor plan of the President's House, much more so than for the initial exterior design, was Leinster House. Hoban's deviations from this example, such as the addition of an oval saloon on the South Front, served to bring that Palladian model up to date stylistically.

Although Seale has tentatively suggested that Hoban, being personally familiar with Leinster House, probably would have followed its example in using a two-story entrance hall, late eighteenth-century Irish homes, such as Lucan House, instead generally featured single-story halls.[25] Hoban did, however, likely follow the example of Leinster House when it came to the East Room, or rather, East Rooms.

Although not a feature of Richard Castle's original plans, by 1759 Leinster House had two "long rooms" on its northern end, on different floors.[26] These first- and second-story rooms, running from front to back of the house, provided the model for Hoban's East Room and are in an analogous location on the overall floor plan. The lower room served as a state dining room and that directly above was a picture gallery.

Hoban probably followed this precedent in his original three-story design by incorporating two East Rooms, one above the other. The one on the first floor would have been the State Dining Room, while the second-floor room, with its Palladian window, would have been George Washington's "Audience Chamber." Here, except on special occasions, only privileged visitors of state would have been admitted.

Other rooms on the first floor were no doubt intended to have more widespread public access. Hoban's oval saloon was surely meant to host President Washington's weekly ceremonial "levees." The adjoining room, directly across the hallway from the service staircase, was probably a breakfast parlor or private dining room, like the equivalent room in the plan of Leinster House.[27]

Following standard eighteenth-century social custom, both of the dining rooms on the first story likely had attached drawing rooms, to which ladies might retire after dinner. This arrangement would create two separate circuits of parlors, one public and one private—explaining the rationale behind the unusual break in the enfilade of Hoban's floor plan. Meanwhile, the room in the northwest corner, isolated from the rest of the house, was probably a library, a suitable space for the president to receive ordinary citizen callers (as was expected in Washington's day).[28]

The second-floor room over the Entrance Hall, behind the stately Ionic columns of the north frontispiece, was the likely location of the president's private study—the equivalent of the modern Oval Office.[29] The Dublin Custom House had a similar arrangement; the boardroom of the Commissioners of Trade was located on the second floor, in the center of the north front.[30] The oval room directly across the hall undoubtedly contained a drawing room for the first lady, as the equivalent space does today. The southwest corner room, then as now, was the logical site of the presidential bedroom, with adjoining dressing rooms.[31] The existence of a third floor makes it probable that, instead of the shared dressing room found in the White House of John Adams's day, Hoban originally followed standard eighteenth-century custom by giving the master and mistress separate dressing rooms.

The third floor would have housed the bedrooms for other residents of the President's House. The flooring in the chambers above the second-story East Room was likely raised up by 3 feet to accommodate a high ceiling in the Audience Chamber below. While found in the White House as built, this idea, too, ultimately derives from Leinster House.[32]

CONCLUSIONS

In reconstructing the facades of Hoban's 1792 design, it is possible to imagine several variants on the same basic exterior, in particular with regard to the North Front centerpiece and rustication. Hoban himself probably presented George Washington with a few different variations. The most likely proposals are shown here. Thus there are two versions of a neoclassical pedimented design, one in Robert Adam's style and another homaging James Gandon. Also presented are several versions of a simpler balustraded North Facade. In the latter drawings, the swags below the windows on the north frontispiece derive from written descriptions and surviving photography of the now-vanished Desart Court.

After reconstructing Hoban's 1792 design as far as possible, one question remains: Why is today's White House so much more stylistically conservative than the initial proposal? The answer almost certainly lies with Hoban's client, George Washington.

A man who grew up among the brick Palladian edifices of colonial Virginia, George Washington was likely unaccustomed to the fashionable neoclassicism of metropolitan Britain and Ireland. Given Washington's recorded preference for ornate stone architecture, he must have asked Hoban to decorate the President's House with carved stone details during their interview. Hoban would have complied, and the initial results, perhaps, left the more traditionalist Washington dismayed. Therefore, in redrafting the White House to use only two stories, Hoban likely took the opportunity to satisfy his client by making his design more conservative in style.

Properly understood, Hoban's 1792 design for the President's House reveals an architect of fashionable taste, considerable talent, and a playful sensibility. That Hoban is routinely dismissed as a throwback to Palladian rigidity of style is likely due to the fact that his best-known building, the modern White House, reflects the conservative taste of his principal patron rather than his own inclinations. Judged by his own architectural style, James Hoban emerges once more as what he truly was: a leading pioneer of the Federal style in postrevolutionary America, who stands to that movement much as Benjamin Henry Latrobe stands to the later "plain style" and the American Greek Revival.

The prevailing misperception of Hoban's architectural style may have so far prevented him from being recognized as the true architect of distinguished buildings elsewhere. In Charleston, for instance, the William Blacklock House, an exquisite Federal home, has a front stoop extraordinarily similar in design to the rear steps of Desart Court. Meanwhile, the Nathaniel Russell House, long recognized as one of the city's finest antebellum houses, has a facade whose second-floor arcade combines the recessed windows of Robert Adam's 20 St. James's Square with the large tripartite keystones of Desart Court's rusticated garden front. Not only that: the Russell House has the owner's initials set as a cipher in the iron railing of its balcony, as at the William Seabrook House. Neither of these houses has any architect verified on record. If James Hoban was indeed the designer of these highly esteemed Federal-era buildings, it is high time that he receives his due recognition.

RECONSTRUCTION OF JAMES HOBAN'S PLANS FOR FLOORS 1–3, WITH INTERIOR WALLS OF BRICK AND STONE

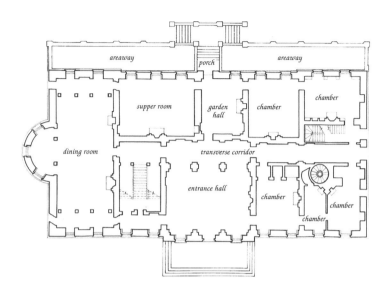

Floor plan of Leinster House as it is today. The second-floor long room above the Supper Room was the Duke of Leinster's picture gallery in the eighteenth century; today it is the meeting chamber of the Senate of Ireland.

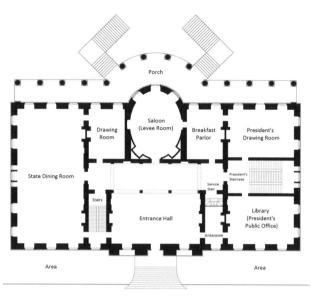

Reconstruction of the intended first-floor plan of James Hoban's 1792 competition design, shown with brick interior walls. It is likely that Hoban would have offered George Washington the option to economize on materials by using brick, at the expense of a certain amount of internal space.

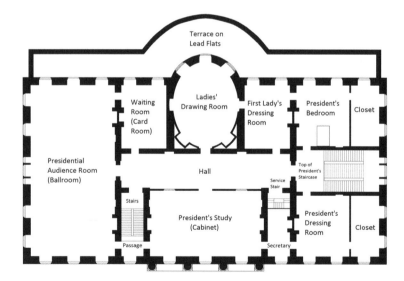

Reconstruction of the second-floor plan of James Hoban's 1792 design, shown with brick interior walls. The lead roof of the rear porch would have served as an open-air gallery for the second story.

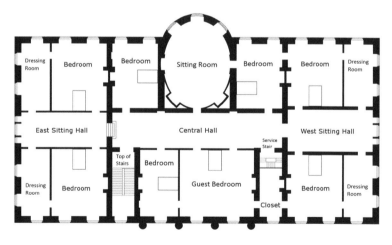

Reconstruction of the third-floor plan of James Hoban's 1792 design, shown with brick interior walls.

RECONSTRUCTION OF JAMES HOBAN'S PLANS FOR FLOORS 1–3, WITH INTERIOR WALLS OF STONE ONLY

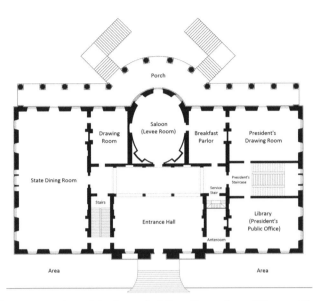

Reconstruction of the intended first-floor plan of James Hoban's 1792 competition design, shown with internal walls made entirely of stone. The enfilade is broken up into two different circuits, one public and one private, each with a drawing room and a dining room.

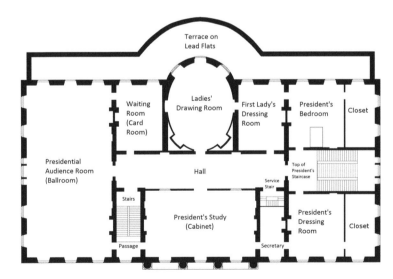

Reconstruction of the second-floor plan of James Hoban's 1792 design, shown with stone interior walls. Starting in the antechamber outside the Audience Room, visitors could proceed in a counterclockwise circuit whose climax was the presidential bedroom. Then as now, the second-floor oval room was meant as a library or drawing room.

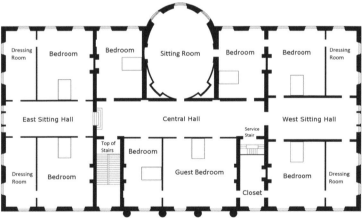

Reconstruction of the third-floor plan of James Hoban's 1792 design, shown with stone interior load-bearing walls. This would have been a chamber story containing numerous bedrooms. The floor of the rooms directly over the Audience Room is raised up by 3 feet (six steps).

NOTES

This essay was first published in *White House History,* no. 42 (Summer 2016): 16–33.

1. William Seale, *The President's House: A History*, 2nd ed. (Washington, D.C.: White House Historical Association, 2008), 1:32.

2. William Ryan and Desmond Guinness, *The White House: An Architectural History* (New York: McGraw-Hill, 1980), 61–62; Seale, *President's House*, 1:34.

3. Charles Bulfinch's copies are preserved in Stephen V. Van Rensselaer to Commissioner Joseph Elgar, Washington, D.C., n.d. [a report for January 1829], Records of the Commissioners for the District of Columbia, Commissioners' Letters Received, Records of the Office of Public Buildings and Grounds, 1791–1867, Record Group 42, National Archives. As of March 14, 2015, they are also digitally archived, and credited to Bulfinch, in the Prints and Photographs Division of the Library of Congress website. See James Hoban's alternative design for the North Portico, "The White House, Washington, D.C., Plan and detail of portico," Library of Congress, www.loc.gov/pictures.

4. This may not be the only case in which Hoban offered his clients a choice as to a pediment or balustrade to crown the principal facade of a public building. William Seale has suggested (*President's House*, 1:13, 34) that Hoban may have designed the Charleston County Courthouse, despite its traditional attribution to the amateur Judge William Drayton. In the 1850s, the local author Charles Fraser mentioned that the original design of the Courthouse apparently included a balustraded parapet: "I had, for a long time, in my portfolio, an original draft of the present building, with all its measurements set down, which differed only in a parapet wall from that which was adopted." See Gene Waddell, *Charleston Architecture, 1670–1860*, (Charleston, S.C.: Wyrick, 2003), 1:124.

5. On Hoban's popularity with the elite of Charleston, see Seale, *President's House*, 1:29.

6. Ibid., 1:45–46; Ryan and Guinness, *White House*, 67–69. Ryan and Guinness note (p. 69) that Benjamin Henry Latrobe, writing in 1817, endorsed this view.

7. James Hoban to the Commissioners for the District of Columbia, Washington, 1792, cited in William Seale, "James Hoban: Builder of the White House," *White House History*, no. 22 (Spring 2008): 7–9.

8. See William Seale, *The White House: The History of an American Idea*, 2nd ed. (Washington, D.C.: White House Historical Association, 2001), 32–33.

9. Edward McParland, *James Gandon: Vitruvius Hibernicus* (London: A. Zwemmer, 1985), 10–13. Gandon's initial design for the County Hall was engraved in John Woolfe and James Gandon, *Vitruvius Britannicus*, vol. 5 (London, 1771).

10. Matthew Baigell argues for Hoban as the bank's architect on the basis of the connection to the Dublin Royal Exchange. Matthew Baigell, "James Hoban and the First Bank of the United States," *Journal of the Society of Architectural Historians* 28, no. 2 (May 1969): 135–36. Kenneth Hafertepe follows the standard attribution to Blodget, but he admits that, if this is true, Blodgett must have borrowed architectural books from Hoban. Kenneth Hafertepe, "Banking Houses in the United States: The First Generation, 1781–1811," *Winterthur Portfolio* 35, no. 1 (Spring 2000): 1–52.

11. For a discussion of the ceiling of the now-destroyed Long Room, see McParland, *James Gandon*, 60–62.

12. The best surviving written description of the exterior of Desart Court is in Thomas U. Sadleir and Page L. Dickinson, *Georgian Mansions in Ireland, With Some Account of the Evolution of Georgian Architecture and Decoration* (Dublin: Dublin University Press, 1916). Sadleir and Dickinson, writing before Desart Court burned in 1922, note (p. 55) that "A few feet above the door, and placed on the projecting entablature, is a carved stone with a scroll supporting a baron's coronet, and bearing the legend 'Anno Don. [*sic*] 1733.'"

13. McParland, *James Gandon*, 58, says of Gandon's work on the Custom House: "Though it is reasonable to refer to this as an example of mannerism, there is no need to discern in it—as is often done in discussions of mannerism—tension or unease. It is complex, and there is an element of wit in it."

14. Robert Adam, *Ruins of the Palace of the Emperor Diocletian at Spalatro in Dalmatia* (London, 1764).

15. The stone blocks of Hoban's rustication were evidently 1 foot high, and the grooves between them were to be

2.25 inches tall apiece. The total internal height of the first floor was 19 feet—ideal for keeping the rooms cool in Washington summer heat.

16. Colen Campbell, *Vitruvius Britannicus*, 3 vols. (London, 1715).
17. Robert Adam and James Adam, *The Works in Architecture of Robert and James Adam*, 2 vols. (London, 1778).
18. David J. Griffin and Simon Lincoln, *Drawings from the Irish Architectural Archive* (Dublin: Irish Architectural Archive, 1993), 27.
19. For a detailed look at this engraving, see Seale, *White House*, 57–58.
20. Presumably Hoban, aware of the government's need for economy as well as Thomas Jefferson's stated preference for brick walls in the competition advertisement, proposed to Washington two alternatives for the internal walls of the house: he could have a house built fully of stone or one with a stone veneer and a brick core. In the latter case, the internal walls would likely be thicker, reducing the dimensions of the rooms. This explains why Hoban's surviving North Front section shows a different wall thickness (3 feet) from his accompanying floor plan (2 feet, 3 inches). The wall section evidently shows window reveals with straight sides, while those in the plan are clearly splayed. The difficulties of juggling two different wall depths no doubt caused Hoban to make the error of accidentally giving his porch's columns too small a diameter.
21. "Building of the Month–August 2013: The Casino at Marino, MARINO Td., Marino, County Dublin," Buildings of Ireland National Inventory of Architectural Heritage website, www.buildingsofireland.
22. This attribution is mentioned in Seale, "James Hoban," 17, and in Ryan and Guinness, *White House*, 95. The Seabrook House features an unusual reversed Imperial stair, like that originally built by Hoban as the White House Grand Stair. In fact, as McParland notes (*James Gandon*, 63), James Gandon executed just such a reversed Imperial stair in marble at the Dublin Custom House in the 1780s.
23. For a drawing of the mask keystone at Desart Court, see Sadleir and Dickinson, *Georgian Mansions*, 54.
24. Seale, "James Hoban," 9.
25. For Seale's comments, see *President's House*, 1:46–47. A good look at Lucan House—whose oval saloon was the likely inspiration for Hoban's oval room—is found in Jacqueline O'Brien and Desmond Guinness, *Great Irish Houses and Castles* (New York: Harry N. Abrams, 1992), 116–19.
26. David J. Griffin and Caroline Pegum, *Leinster House, 1744–2000: An Architectural History* (Dublin: Irish Architectural Archive, 2000), 31.
27. Today this space is the Red Room. However, John Adams is known to have used it as a dining room.
28. Washington himself likely asked Hoban to designate a first-floor office space, separate from his own private study upstairs. This was the arrangement found at his New York residence. When Washington moved into Robert Morris's Market Street house in Philadelphia, citizen callers had to ascend to the third floor to reach the public office that housed the presidential secretaries. Washington complained heatedly about this fact in his letters. See Edward Lawler Jr., "The President's House Revisited," The President's House in Philadelphia website, www.ushistory.org/presidentshouse.
29. While the original oval rooms evidently had false windows with mirrored sashes at the north end, the president's study probably had two internal windows set in the room's south wall, which would have provided light to the upstairs central corridor.
30. McParland, *James Gandon*, 62–63.
31. At Leinster House, the Duchess of Leinster's dressing room and bedroom occupied the equivalent space.
32. Griffin and Pegum, *Leinster House*, 67.

VII. MATTHEW R. COSTELLO

Building the President's House with Enslaved Labor: James Hoban and Slavery

In several ways, James Hoban's life resembles the classic immigrant success story. Born to a modest family in County Kilkenny, Ireland, Hoban studied at the Dublin Society School of Architectural Drawing before seeking greater opportunities abroad. He had arrived in the new United States by 1785 and was settled in Charleston, South Carolina, by 1787, where he and his business partner Pierce Purcell worked on a variety of building projects. In other ways, Hoban's experiences were very American. During his time in Charleston, he purchased at least one enslaved man and learned the benefits of slave ownership—lessons he took with him to the new Federal City, where he amassed his fortune through public and private construction. Enslaved workers played a vital role not only in building the President's House and the Capitol Building but also in Hoban's rise to prominence and prosperity in early Washington, D.C.

As with any study that explores the experiences of enslaved communities, documentation is scant and often incomplete. Most slave owners did not teach enslaved people how to read or write, and over time states passed laws that made these acts illegal; thus there are few surviving written sources. In addition to these general limitations, it is believed that all of Hoban's personal papers were destroyed in a fire sometime during the 1880s. All that remains to document his life are those written in a professional capacity, which reveal little about Hoban's views on slavery. However, surviving payroll and census records, advertisements, and newspapers do shed light on Hoban's relationship with slavery and its evolution during his lifetime. While their stories might be lost or incomplete, enslaved people were crucial to his success, much like the enslaved workers who built the President's House were to the Commissioners for the District of Columbia.

Hoban arrived in Charleston in early 1787. At some point, he purchased an enslaved man named Peter. According to a 1789 advertisement published in the *City Gazette*, Peter, who was "by trade a carpenter," had "absented himself" shortly after the New Year. Hoban sought his immediate return and offered a reward of 20 shillings, warning that anyone who harbored or carried Peter away would be "dealt with according to law."[1] Two years later, Hoban was likely involved in work to prepare Charleston's Exchange Building for the upcoming visit of the country's most prominent citizen–President George Washington. During his visit, the president did meet with affluent citizens who later vouched for Hoban's abilities as a builder and project manager.[2]

In March 1792, the commissioners for the Federal District announced a design competition for the public buildings. In June, Hoban set off for Philadelphia to discuss his ideas with the president. The following month, Hoban's plans for the President's House were selected by the commissioners with Washington's approval.[3] The laying of the cornerstone took place on October 13, 1792, and construction picked up the following spring. However, these building projects quickly faced labor shortages as there were few free workers to be had: wages were low, and rations and housing for them were wholly inadequate. As the commissioners struggled to recruit laborers, it became increasingly clear that enslaved workers could help meet their demands. Hired out by local slave owners, enslaved laborers cleared the land, cut down trees, removed stumps, quarried and transported stone, and made thousands of bricks. There were also some enslaved craftsmen, and the names of four are known–Peter, Ben, Harry, and Daniel. Their names appear on a May 1795 carpenters' payroll, and their wages were signed for by James Hoban. In that month alone, Peter and Ben each worked twenty-eight days, and their labor was valued at £10 10s each. Daniel worked twenty-five days, worth £6 and 5s; Harry nine days, worth £2 5s.[4] Perhaps Hoban permitted these men to keep small sums of their earnings, as this was not uncommon at the time; however, most slave owners simply pocketed the wages for themselves.

With the name "Peter" appearing in both the *City Gazette* advertisement and the carpenters' payrolls, it may well be that this Peter was one and the same. Hoban had likely trained Peter to work in his flourishing construction business, and he may have had similar relationships with Ben, Daniel, and Harry, as they all worked at the President's House. In late 1797, after white workers protested their wages and the pay of skilled black workers, the commissioners ordered that "no Negro Carpenters or apprentices be hired at either of the public buildings."[5] While Hoban's enslaved carpenters were banned from the site, he continued overseeing construction until 1800, when President John Adams moved into the White House. According to that year's census, there were four enslaved people living in the Hoban household.[6] While their age and sex were not recorded, these four residents may have been Peter, Ben, Daniel, and Harry.

A few newspaper advertisements illuminate another important aspect of Hoban's relationship with slavery, as he not only profited from enslaved labor but also sold enslaved people. In September 1804, he published an advertisement in the *Washington National Intelligencer* to sell "A Valuable Strong active Negro Man" on behalf of the owner who was not "a resident of the city." Parties interested in "the terms of sale" were instructed to contact "James Hoban, who on application will make them known." Less than a year later, Hoban placed another advertisement in the same newspaper: "For Sale, A Negro Woman and her three Children, the eldest of whom is nine years of age, and the youngest three; the woman is about 33 years old. For further particulars enquire of Captain Hoban."[7] There are two scenarios that explain the second advertisement: either Hoban was not their owner but was selling enslaved people on behalf of someone else, or he was their owner and looking to sell this woman and her young children. Either way, these advertisements suggest that Hoban not only purchased but also sold enslaved people.

The census records toward the end of Hoban's life reveal the peak of his participation in the institution of slavery. In 1820, there were twenty individuals in the Hoban household, nine of whom were enslaved.[8] The nearly equal split between black and white residents was not uncommon for the time, but the number of enslaved people was remarkably large as most households in Washington only had a few enslaved servants. This made Hoban one of the wealthiest slave-owning residents in Ward 2, but in a surprising twist by 1830 there were only two enslaved people and one free woman of color present at the Hoban residence.[9] This record, coupled with Hoban's signing of a petition advocating for the gradual abolition of slavery in 1828,[10] have led some scholars to argue that Hoban began questioning the morality and necessity of slavery. This was not in fact the case.

In April 1832, the executors of Hoban's estate, James Hoban Jr. and Thomas Carbery, placed an advertisement in the *Daily National Intelligencer* to sell two women, five men, and one young child: "These negroes were the property of the late Captain James Hoban, who has directed, by his will, that they shall not be sold or taken out of the District."[11] The discrepancy between the 1830 census and this advertisement means that six enslaved people were not within the household when that was recorded, and based on the ages and the note that some were "good house servants," Hoban may have been hiring them out elsewhere. His request to keep these eight enslaved people within the District does suggest that Hoban did not want to deliberately separate family members from one another; however, this advertisement undermines the notion that Hoban became uncomfortable with slavery toward the end of his life.

On June 8, 1792, President George Washington wrote the following in a letter to the Commissioners for the District of Columbia: "The bearer of this, Mr James Hoben, was strongly recommended to me by Colo. Laurens and sevral other Gentlemen of So. Carolinia when I was there last year, as a person who had made architecture his study, and was well qualified not only for planning or designing buildings, but to superintend the execution of them."[13] Hoban's contemporaries were impressed by his architectural talents and managerial skills, so much so that they relayed these sentiments to President Washington. As an effective builder, this meant that Hoban was well-equipped to supervise both free and enslaved laborers, and likely his experiences as an architect, freemason, carpenter, and slave owner prepared him to manage such a workforce in the nation's capital. Ultimately, Hoban's legacy as the architect of the White House is secure, but it is worth noting that it took many hands—free and enslaved, skilled and unskilled—to bring his vision to life.[14]

NOTES

1. *Charleston City Gazette*, January 17, 1789; *Charleston City Gazette*, April 17, 1790.
2. William Seale, *The President's House: A History*, 2nd ed. (Washington, D.C.: White House Historical Association, 2008), 1:40–51. After Hoban was announced as the winner of the design competition for the President's House, one Charleston newspaper reported that Hoban had indeed met Washington in 1791. See *Charleston City Gazette*, August 9, 1792. Washington never recorded meeting Hoban in Charleston, but it is certainly possible that they met.
3. George Washington to the Commissioners for the District of Columbia, June 8, 1792, *The Papers of George Washington, Presidential Series*, vol. 10, *1 March 1792–15 August 1792*, ed. Robert F. Haggard and Mark A. Mastromarino (Charlottesville: University of Virginia Press, 2002), 439–40, available on *Founders Online* website, www.founders.archives.gov. According to this letter, Hoban was recommended to Washington by "Colo. Laurens and sevral other Gentlemen of So. Carolinia when I was there last year."
4. President's House Carpenters Roll for May 1795, Commissioners Records, Record Group 42, National Ar-

chives, Washington, D.C. See also Seale, *President's House*, 1:26–37; Robert J. Kapsch, "The Labor History of the Construction and Reconstruction of the White House, 1793–1817" (PhD diss., University of Maryland College Park, 1993), 111, 151.

5. Bob Arnebeck, *Slave Labor in the Capital: Building Washington's Iconic Federal Landmarks* (Charleston, S.C.: History Press, 2014), 107–09, 159–61; Lina Mann, "Building the White House," White House Historical Association website, www.whitehousehistory.org.

6. Second Census of the United States, 1800, Washington, District of Columbia, series M32, roll 5, p. 882, image 33, Family History Library Film 6697, Records of the Bureau of the Census, Record Group 29, National Archives.

7. *Washington National Intelligencer,* September 12, 1804; *Washington National Intelligencer*, February 4, 1805.

8. Fourth Census of the United States, 1820, Washington Ward 2, District of Columbia, series M33, roll 5, p. 77, image 84, Records of the Bureau of the Census, Record Group 29, National Archives.

9. Fifth Census of the United States, 1830, Washington Ward 2, Washington, District of Columbia, series M19, roll 14, p. 87, Family History Library Film 0006699, Records of the Bureau of the Census, Record Group 29, National Archives.

10. *Memorial of Inhabitants of the District of Columbia, Praying for the Gradual Abolition of Slavery in the District of Columbia, March 24, 1828* (Washington, D.C.: Gales & Seaton, 1828), available online on the Library of Congress website, www.loc.gov. See also William B. Bushong, "Imagining James Hoban: Portraits of a Master Builder," *White House History*, no. 22 (Spring 2008): 48–57.

11. *Daily National Intelligencer*, April 7, 1832; James Hoban, will and testament, January 3, 1832, District of Columbia Probate Records, 1801–1930, Register of Wills, 1826–1837, 393–94.

12. Thomas Smallwood, *A Narrative of Thomas Smallwood, (Coloured Man:) Giving an Account of His Birth—The Period He Was Held in Slavery—His Release—and Removal to Canada, etc., Together with an Account of the Underground Railroad, Written by Himself* (Toronto: Smallwood; James Stephens, 1851), 46–47. Penelope Fergison, a graduate student at the University of California's Price School and summer intern for the White House Historical Association, discovered this reference in her research on slave patrols in Washington, D.C.

13. George Washington to the Commissioners for the District of Columbia, June 8, 1792, available on *Founders Online* website, www.founders.archives.gov.

14. Note from Matthew Costello: In the first printing of this book, I concluded this chapter by suggesting that Hoban may have been involved with the death of an enslaved man based on the recollection of Thomas Smallwood, a formerly enslaved man who lived and worked in Washington, D.C. New research leads provided by Denis Bergin and Jonathan Pliska helped me discover new evidence that the individual involved was likely an Irish-born man named James Maher, who worked as the principal gardener for the government. For more details on the incident in question, see *Madisonian for the Country*, May 15, 1839, and *Alexandria Gazette*, May 15, 1839.

VIII. KRISTEN HUNTER MASON

James Hoban and the Early Roman Catholic Church in the Federal City of Washington

Well known are James Hoban's significant contributions to the architectural landscape of the Federal City of Washington through his designs, especially for the President's House but also for private houses, and for his supervision of some parts of the building of the U.S. Capitol. The accomplished architect also made a mark in the political arena, serving on the District of Columbia's Common Council, an early iteration of D.C. City Council, for eight years, and on the city's Board of Aldermen for six years.[1] He was also associated with founding Washington's first Freemason Lodge, which is still in operation today as Federal Lodge No. 1.[2] Perhaps less known, however, is Hoban's significant involvement in growing the Roman Catholic Church in the capital city.

Soon after his arrival in Washington in 1792, Hoban became a part of a group of influential Catholic men who helped establish the first churches in the city. These included Daniel Carroll of Duddington,[3] James Barry, Notley Young, Mayor Robert Brent, and the Reverend William Matthews. They were concerned for the spiritual lives of the men coming to Washington to work on the various building projects, some with their families. Near the President's House, in 1794 Hoban helped found the first church of any denomination in the Federal City, St. Patrick's Church, and he stayed committed to it in the coming decades, constructing a new church building in 1809 and later expanding it and adding the Washington Catholic Seminary building in 1815. Near Capitol Hill, Hoban built St. Mary's Chapel in 1806, and in 1820 he contributed to the founding of the second Catholic church in the city, St. Peter's Church. James Hoban's involvement in fostering several Catholic institutions in the city for the benefit of his fellow Irishmen reveals his benevolent nature and the significant role his Catholic faith played in his life.

JAMES HOBAN'S CATHOLIC ROOTS

Hoban's interest in growing the Catholic Church in America can perhaps find its origin in his childhood in Ireland as the son of tenant farmers. Ireland during the eighteenth century was marked by harsh Penal Laws designed by the Anglo-Protestant ruling class to strip Catholics of their rights and suppress their faith. These laws, first going into effect in the 1690s, excluded three-fourths of the Irish population of 4 million from the political process, banning Catholics from holding public office, voting, and inheriting and buying land. Because these laws also severely restricted how Catholics could practice their faith, there were very few Roman Catholic churches during this period and most of the faithful worshipped in their homes. The Penal Laws began to be slowly relaxed in 1778, around the time Hoban was beginning his training in Dublin. This attempted suppression of Catholicism in Ireland, however, reinforced Irish Catholics' devotion to their faith and intertwined their religion with their cultural identity.[4] Hoban, coming from this environment, would have been proud of his Catholic faith and Irish culture.

While religion was a large aspect of his life in Ireland, it proved even more important to Hoban as an immigrant in America. The Catholic Church acted as a central institution for immigrants, providing a community on which newcomers could rely for help in making connections and establishing themselves in their new cities. It also served as a familiar link to Ireland, through which it acted as a means of preserving cultural identity.[5] Additionally, since proper church buildings and formal parishes were scarce in Ireland due to laws against Catholic worship, religious toleration in the United States gave Irish immigrants opportunities for worship and religious formation that they had not previously had, and they cherished them.

This devotion to his faith is evident in Hoban's immediate involvement in the Catholic community in Charleston. When he arrived in the city, likely around 1787, he would have found a small but tightly knit group of Irish Catholic settlers. Prior to the American Revolution, Catholicism had not been tolerated in the Carolinas, and in fact had been outlawed in 1696, and the few Catholic settlers in those colonies kept their religion secret. But during the revolutionary era, religious toleration gained ground, and even before freedom of worship was enshrined in the First Amendment to the Constitution, these Catholics came together to form parishes. Hoban, along with his business partner Pierce Purcell and his family, were part of a small group that formed St. Mary's Church in 1788 in Charleston. Hoban and Purcell, by this time respected builders and members of the Charleston community, likely helped raise the funds to purchase the property for the church in 1789.[6]

HOBAN ESTABLISHES THE CHURCH IN THE FEDERAL CITY:
ST. PATRICK'S PARISH

It is clear that Hoban carried this interest in his faith with him when he moved to the Federal City in 1792, to begin construction of the President's House. In gathering supplies and a labor force, he encouraged many Irishmen to come to Washington, promising them plentiful work throughout the city on the various building projects. Many of these Irishmen worked as the carpenters and craftsmen on the President's House, and they set up living quarters, often just simple huts, near the construction site. Hoban soon saw that his Irish workers, and their families, were in need of a church that would provide the spiritual, physical, and moral support they were lacking. Holy Trinity Church, in Georgetown, the only Catholic parish at the time in the vicinity, was too far away for the workers and their families to attend.[7]

Likely around 1793, Hoban petitioned Bishop John Carroll of Baltimore for the creation of a new parish located near the President's House. With the approval of the bishop, it is believed that Hoban asked the Reverend Anthony Caffry, a Dominican priest from Dublin, to be the pastor of the new church. It is possible that Bishop Carroll, acquainted with Fr. Caffry, recommended the priest to Hoban. While there is no record of Hoban's appeal to Fr. Caffry, it is documented that Fr. Caffry had settled in the Federal City of Washington by January 1794. Fr. Caffry and possibly Hoban together decided to name the new parish in honor of Ireland's primary patron saint, St. Patrick, a name befitting the Irish congregants for whom the church was created.[8]

In April 1794, Fr. Caffry wrote to the Commissioners for the District of Columbia seeking land on which to build the church: "St. Patrick's Church would make the town exceedingly pleasing and familiar to a great number of my countrymen and persuasion."[9] A few days later, two lots in city square 376, bounded by Ninth, Tenth, F, and G Streets NW, were purchased. The parish was officially established, and the Irish Catholic laborers, with Hoban among them, finally celebrated Mass in their new church, a simple wooden structure. This was the first church of any denomination in Washington City.[10]

While Hoban had been married at and had attended Mass at Holy Trinity, he became one of the early parishioners of St. Patrick's Church and remained active in the church he founded. When Fr. Caffry returned to Ireland in 1804, Hoban found another ally even more committed to growing the church in the Reverend William Matthews. Fr. Matthews, the first American ordained to the Catholic priesthood, became a highly influential figure in the Catholic community in Washington, D.C., and remained pastor at St. Patrick's until 1854. With the ever-increasing numbers of parishioners, St. Patrick's soon outgrew its small wooden church. Fr. Matthews purchased eight more lots adjacent to the church property and, as tradition holds, called upon James Hoban to design and construct a larger church for the parish. Completed in June 1809, St. Patrick's new church, attributed to Hoban, was a simple brick, rectangular building that resembled the medieval church in Callan, County Kilkenny, Ireland, where Hoban grew up.

Because the Catholic Church was still gaining its footing in the United States due to recent persecution in the colonial era, there were very few Catholic churches in the country and the few parishes that did exist worshipped in simple wooden buildings. Designing St. Patrick's after the typical Irish country church would have been a calculated move on Hoban's part to give his Irish laborers, and would-be parishioners, a building that they would immediately recognize from their homeland.[11] The growing congregation soon became more than just a parish of laborers, as some of the city's prominent Catholic families joined. Hoban's simple church had become the prominent place of worship in the capital city in a few short years and would be known as "The Mother Church of Washington."[12]

ST. PATRICK'S GROWS: WASHINGTON CATHOLIC SEMINARY

The growth of St. Patrick's Church continued, and in 1815, Hoban was again called upon to expand his brick church and add a school building. Fr. Matthews had given an adjacent plot of land, which he had personally purchased, to the Jesuits of Georgetown to create a seminarian house away from Georgetown College's main campus. In return Fr. Matthews was hoping to receive assistance in his parochial duties from these resident Jesuits. The Jesuits, with the assistance of Fr. Matthews, hired James Hoban to design and build the new school building, and Fr. Matthews requested that the church be expanded as well.[13] Hoban's role was recorded in a letter by John McElroy, a Jesuit seminarian at the time, who wrote on May 4, 1815, that "the Building of our Noviceship will commence in a day or two. Capt Hoban is the Architect appointed to carry on the Building."[14] More than a year later, on August 31, 1816, an article in the *Washington Daily National Intelligencer* listed the ongoing building project as "an extensive Catholic Seminary, and the Catholic Chapel considerably enlarged."[15] A watercolor of the church from the 1830s and a later photograph of the school building record Hoban's completed work on the church complex. To enlarge the church, Hoban added two wings off the central altar area, transforming the rectangular building into the traditional cruciform shape typical of Roman Catholic Churches. The church ran parallel to F Street with its entrance on Tenth Street and measured about 120 by 85 feet.[16] The resemblance to St. Mary's is even more apparent in this enlarged church than in Hoban's first design. The brick school building appears to be in a simple Federal style that would have resembled many other buildings in the city while also nicely complementing the style of St. Patrick's next door.

The building was finished in 1817 and used as a private lay school for boys until 1820 while the Jesuits still made preparations for the seminary. In 1820, the Jesuits took over and reorganized the boys' school to become the Washington Catholic Seminary; it officially opened on September 8, 1821. The school became widely successful, and many prominent citizens of Washington, Protestant and Catholic alike, enrolled their sons, among them Daniel Webster and Commodore John Rodgers. President John Quincy Adams even attended the closing exercises in 1825 at the request of Fr. Matthews.[17]

Among the first class of students enrolled in 1821 was Hoban's own son, 13-year-old James Hoban Jr. A history of the school records that during the first annual closing exercises, on July 27, 1822, young Hoban "literally swept all before him in his college classes, and received, besides an extra premium for general excellence."[18] This James Hoban, eventually a prestigious attorney in Washington, D.C., also sent his son, James Hoban III, to the school during the 1840s. Another of the architect's sons, Henry, was a student at the school, enrolling in 1827. Henry Hoban was ordained a Jesuit priest in 1852 and served between 1856 and 1865 as the vice president of the school, then reorganized as Gonzaga College but still housed in the original building built by his father.[19]

THE CHURCH ON CAPITOL HILL: ST. MARY'S CHAPEL AND ST. PETER'S CHURCH

Hoban's involvement in the growing Catholic Church in Washington, D.C., was not confined to St. Patrick's Parish; his commitment to the mission spread throughout the city. Around 1800, Hoban and the other prominent local Catholics saw the need for another church near the Capitol building site to serve the Irish Catholics working there. St. Patrick's, like Holy Trinity before it, was too far away for Catholics on Capitol Hill and living across the Potomac River to attend. Hoban and a committee started a subscription to raise funds for the church. In an 1801 letter to Bishop Carroll, Notley Young, a member of the committee, stated that "the petitioners have unanimously assured me that three thousand dollars can be immediately collected for this purpose from Catholic gentlemen who reside within or about the [Navy] Yard . . . and this sum, according to the calculations of Capt. Hoban, is nearly sufficient to complete the building." Unfortunately, the subscriptions fell short, as the thirty-five donors, including James Hoban, managed to raise only $1,060.[20]

However, around the same time, James Barry, another prominent Catholic of the District of Columbia and a member of the subscription committee for the new church, had been planning to construct a small family chapel on his estate near the Navy Yard in Southeast Washington. Barry had hired James Hoban, his friend and sometime business associate, to design and oversee the building of the chapel. A September 1801 letter from Bishop Carroll to Barry detailed that Hoban had estimated the cost of the chapel to be $2,000.[21] When Barry saw that there were insufficient funds for the new church for the Capitol Hill neighborhood, he directed that his family chapel be made instead into a chapel to be used by the community. The philanthropic Barry, however, found himself unable to fully finance the project, so Daniel Carroll stepped in and paid the major share of the building costs. Carroll's contribution and the extent of Hoban's involvement are recorded in an account entry for the building of the chapel in which it is noted that Carroll paid Hoban $70 on July 8, 1806 for "plan & attendg. Building." The same entry also includes a payment of $820 to a G. Coombs for "bill of building church."[22]

Completed in 1806, St. Mary's Chapel, locally referred to as Barry's Chapel, robustly served the community for several years. By 1811, however, Barry, his wife, and two daughters all tragically died from tuberculosis, and the chapel fell into disrepair. Mass was sporadically celebrated at the chapel until about 1819, and the chapel was eventually demolished. The engraved cornerstone of the chapel designed by Hoban survives today in an outer wall of the Holy Name Chapel of St. Dominic's Church in Southwest Washington, D.C.[23]

While St. Mary's provided a temporary place of worship for the faithful in Southeast Washington and the Capitol Hill area, the need for a true parish was again made apparent by the new influx of Irish Catholic workers coming to rebuild the city following its burning by British troops in 1814. Hoban and the group that had attempted to form a parish in 1801 renewed their efforts, and Daniel Carroll donated land for the proposed church on C Street SE. This time Hoban and the committee were able to raise the necessary funds, and St. Peter's Church, the second Catholic parish in Washington, was formed in September 1821.[24] As a member of the founding committee, Hoban may have had a hand in designing St. Peter's first church building. The Reverend James F. M. Lucas, the first pastor of the church, mentioned in a letter to Archbishop Ambrose Marechal of Baltimore, in September 1821, that "the Irish gentlemen seem very content and wish me to relieve them of the burden of constructions etc, because the members of the committee do not get on very well, some favoring one plan, others another and some have resigned."[25] It is conceivable that one of these debated plans was Hoban's own design. Whether his plans for the church were actually adopted and built remains unknown.

CATHOLICISM IN WASHINGTON, D.C.: HOBAN'S OTHER LEGACY

When James Hoban died on December 8, 1831, his obituary did not state the location of his funeral or burial. However, given his strong affiliation and devotion to St. Patrick's, it is likely that his funeral Mass was celebrated at the church by Fr. Matthews in the building Hoban himself had designed and built. It is not documented where he was originally buried, but historians have noted, based on oral and Hoban family tradition, that he was interred next to his wife and two daughters, who predeceased him, in St. Patrick's cemetery.[26] By 1831, however, St. Patrick's had two cemetery locations: one in the immediate churchyard along the north side of its lot on F Street, and the other, an auxiliary cemetery, located outside the city boundaries on today's Florida Avenue, between First and Second Streets

NE. The land for this cemetery was donated by Ann Casanave, daughter of Notley Young, to Fr. Matthews in 1808 for the use of all Catholics in Washington, but was mostly used by St. Patrick's. After 1810, with its churchyard cemetery running out of space, St. Patrick's buried most of its parishioners in this auxiliary location. It is possible that the Hoban family members, with Susana dying in 1822, were placed here.[27]

Around 1863, however, St. Patrick's removed its churchyard cemetery to make way for a larger church building and sold the land of the auxiliary location. Many of those buried in these cemeteries were reinterred at the newly opened Mount Olivet Cemetery in the Northeast section of the city.[28] It is recorded that Marion Hoban, the wife of James Hoban Jr., bought a plot for the family at Mount Olivet in 1863, and it is believed that the Hoban family burials were all moved to this location at that time.[29] It is here that the Hoban family still rests today.

Hoban's involvement with Washington's Catholic Church left an enduring legacy for the city. He helped give Catholics places to worship and to learn—something he likely never dreamed possible, growing up in Ireland where his faith was suppressed. His contributions to establishing a strong Roman Catholic Church in Washington continue to benefit Catholics today.

NOTES

1. William W. Warner, *At Peace with All Their Neighbors: Catholics and Catholicism in the National Capital, 1787–1860* (Washington, D.C.: Georgetown University Press, 1994), 161.
2. It should be noted that Hoban's involvement with the Freemasons was short-lived and its time frame perhaps reflects a clear motive of utilizing the connections available within the group to establish himself in Charleston and Washington. There is evidence that he joined the Masons first in Charleston and transferred his membership the lodge in Georgetown when he moved to Washington in 1792. A year later, he and several other members living in the District came together to create Federal Lodge No. 1. Only a few years later, however, in 1799, Hoban's name is gone from the Freemasons' rolls. By this time Hoban had married and had become increasing involved in the Roman Catholic Church in Washington. It should also be noted that membership in the Freemasons is strictly forbidden for Catholics and this prohibition was likely another reason for Hoban's short-lived ties with the group. Details of Hoban's involvement in the Freemasons are in "James Hoban, the Architect and Builder of the White House and the Superintendent of the Building of the Capitol at Washington," *American Catholic Historical Researches*, 3, no. 1 (January 1907), 39–40; "History of Federal Lodge No. 1," Federal Lodge No. 1 website, www.federallodge.org; Kenton N. Harper, *History of the Grand Lodge and of Freemasonry in the District of Columbia* (Washington, D.C.: R. Beresford, 1911), 173–75.
3. The Daniel Carroll discussed in this essay is of the Duddington branch of the Carroll family and not to be confused with the Daniel Carroll of the Carrollton branch, who was a Signer of the Articles of Confederation and the Constitution. Duddington refers to the family's estate, which occupied the land in Southwest Washington where the Capitol complex now sits.
4. Thomas Bartlett, *Ireland: A History* (Cambridge: Cambridge University Press, 2010), 145, 163–64, 178.
5. Kevin Kenny, *The American Irish: A History* (Harlow, U.K.: Pearson Education, 2000), 71–75.
6. Thomas F. Hopkins, "St. Mary's Church, Charleston, S.C.: The First Catholic Church in the Original Diocese of Charleston," *Year Book 1897* (Charleston, S.C.: Walker Evans, & Cogswell, 1897), 430–35; "Our History," St. Mary of the Annunciation Catholic Church website, www.sma.church.
7. John V. Hinkel, "St. Patrick's: Mother Church of Washington," *Records of the Columbia Historical Society* 57–59 (1957–59): 33–34.
8. Ibid., 34; Warner, *At Peace,* 100. Hoban's relationship with the Reverend Anthony Caffry has been passed down in local histories and is commemorated on the plaque outside St. Patrick Church, though no historical evidence has

been found to document that they knew each other before Fr. Caffry was pastor. Unfortunately, Hoban's papers burned after his death.

9. Rev. Anthony Caffry to the Commissioners, April 14, 1794, Records of the Commissioners for the District of Columbia, Record Group 42, National Archives, Washington, D.C., Letters Received, quoted in Warner, *At Peace*, 100.

10. "St. Patrick's Church, Washington," *American Catholic Historical Researches* 1, no. 1 (January 1905): 64; Warner, *At Peace*, 101; Hinkel, "St. Patrick's," 43.

11. Hoban's St. Patrick's Church is often referred to as in the Gothic Revival style. This style, however, is not formally recognized by historians as present in the United States until the 1840s, decades after Hoban built the church. Comparisons of period drawings and the extant ruins of St. Mary's Church in Callan, County Kilkenny, to the images we have of Hoban's St. Patrick's reveal a strong resemblance. See the image catalog for the photographs and further discussion of the similarities. While historians do not classify American architecture from before 1840 as Gothic Revival style, Hoban's St. Patrick's may be a sort of proto–Gothic Revival, as it is clearly derived from St. Mary's, which was built during the sixteenth century in the original Gothic style. It also should be noted that St. Mary's in Charleston did not build its formal church until after 1800, well after Hoban had left the city, and he would have attended Mass in the church's simple wooden building.

12. Fr. Paul Liston, "A Short History of St. Patrick Parish," St. Patrick's Catholic Church website, www.saintpatrickdc.org; Charles H. Wentz, ed., *Inventory of Records of St. Patrick's Church and School* (Washington, D.C.: Historical Records Survey Division, 1941), 2; "Notice," *Washington National Intelligencer,* June 30, 1809, 2; Warner, *At Peace*, 103; Hinkel, "St. Patrick's," 43. Just as Hoban's personal invitation to Fr. Caffry to come to America, the hiring of Hoban to build the brick church in 1809 unfortunately remains only part of tradition, as the historical evidence is still undiscovered.

13. Wentz, *Inventory of Records of St. Patrick's*, 13; Warner, *At Peace*, 106.

14. Rev. John McElroy to Rev. Mr. Carey, May 4, 1815, box 58, folder 4, Maryland Province Archives at the Booth Family Center for Special Collections, Georgetown University, Washington, D.C.

15. "The City of Washington," *Washington Daily National Intelligencer*, August 31, 1816, 3.

16. Morris J. MacGregor, *A Parish for the Federal City: St. Patrick's in Washington, 1794–1994.* (Washington, D.C.: Catholic University Press, 1994), 48.

17. Wentz, *Inventory of Records of St. Patrick's*, 14; Warner, *At Peace*, 106–07;

18. Gonzaga College, *An Historical Sketch: From Its Foundation in 1921* (Washington, D.C.: Gonzaga College, 1922), 28.

19. Ibid., 43, 56; "Gonzaga College," *Woodstock Letters* 19, no. 1 (February 1, 1890): 7.

20. Letter quoted in "History," Saint Peter's Church on Capitol Hill website, www.saintpetersdc.org. See also John Gilmary Shea, *Life and Times of the Most Rev. John Carroll, Bishop and First Archbishop of Baltimore* (New York: Edward O. Jenkins' Sons, 1888), 515; Warner, *At Peace*, 108–09, 258.

21. Warner, *At Peace*, 258.

22. Ibid., 110, 182, 270.

23. "From the Norfolk Herald," *Washington Spirit of 'Seventy-Six*, October 12, 1810, 4; "Relic of the First Catholic Chapel in Washington, D.C. 1806," *American Catholic Historical Researches* 13, no. 1 (January 1896): 27.

24. Warner, *At Peace*, 111; "History," St. Peter's Church on Capitol Hill website.

25. Letter quoted in "History," St. Peter's Church on Capitol Hill website.

26. *Washington National Intelligencer*, December 9, 1831; "James Hoban, Builder and Architect of the White House," 47.

27. MacGregor, *A Parish for the Federal City*, 38; "The Old Burial Grounds," *Washington Evening Star*, April 14, 1888, 2; Susana Hoban's obituary, *Washington National Intelligencer*, September 4, 1822.

28. MacGregor, *A Parish for the Federal City*, 190; Anne O. Brockett, *Gone But Not Forgotten: Cemeteries in the Nation's Capital* (Washington, D.C.: District of Columbia Historic Preservation Office, 2012), 14; Warner, *At Peace*, 111, 258.

29. Transcription of available records pertaining to the Hoban family provided through e-mail by Cheryl Tyiska, Mount Olivet Cemetery.

Catalog

I

Irish Influences

James Hoban was born in 1755 in the agricultural world of County Kilkenny, Ireland. His parents, Edward and Martha Bayne Hoban, were tenant farmers on the Cuffe family's Desart Court estate just outside of Callan. Hoban birthplace, a thatch-roof whitewashed stone cottage, stood until it was demolished in the mid-1930s. It resembled the one seen opposite and was typical of rural-class housing at the time.

Hoban likely received training as a carpenter and wheelwright in the workshops of Desart Court during his teenage years. It was here that he acquired the basic skills and his eye for design and construction that would serve him during his long career as a builder. The influence of Irish architecture Hoban knew in his youth, including Desart Court and the surrounding country houses, is evident in the designs he later executed in America.

IRISH INFLUENCES

Desart Court

Desart Court was built by John Cuffe soon after he was made First Baron Desart in 1733. The Cuffe family descended from Joseph Cuffe, a soldier in Oliver Cromwell's army. They established their seat at Castle Inch in the mid-1600s, and their move to Desart Court signaled the baron's elevation in status.

The design of Desart Court is attributed to Sir Edward Lovett Pearce, who also designed Parliament House in Dublin. The grand Palladian country house was built of blue limestone and featured a central block with pavilions on either side. A similar orientation is reflected in James Hoban's late eighteenth-century design for the President's House in the Federal City of Washington.

Tragically, along with more than two-hundred country houses belonging to the Anglo-Irish aristocracy, Desart Court was burned by the antitreaty faction during the Irish Civil War in February 1922. Although soon rebuilt, the house was permanently demolished in 1957.

Hoban's 1792 design for the North Front of the President's House bears a striking resemblance to the Garden Front of Desart Court. His first entry into the competition for the design of the President's House, which was ultimately adjusted, included Desart Court's pedimented colonnade raised over a high ground-floor basement with the columns reaching over the second and third floors.

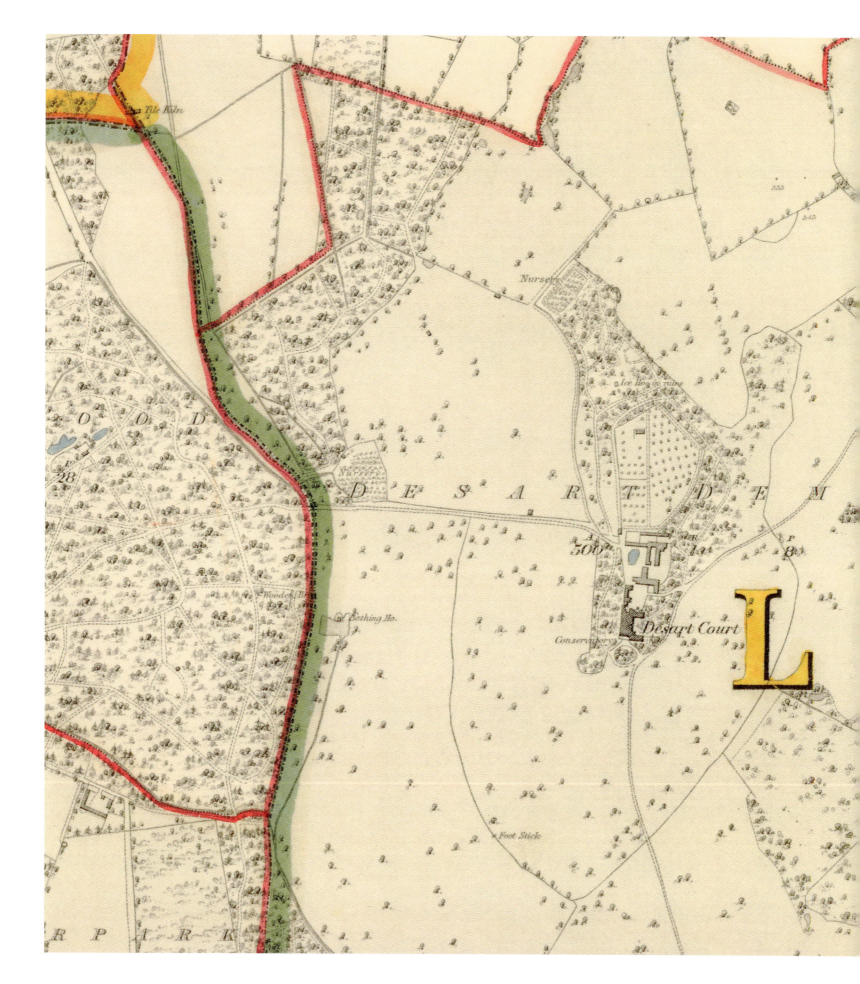

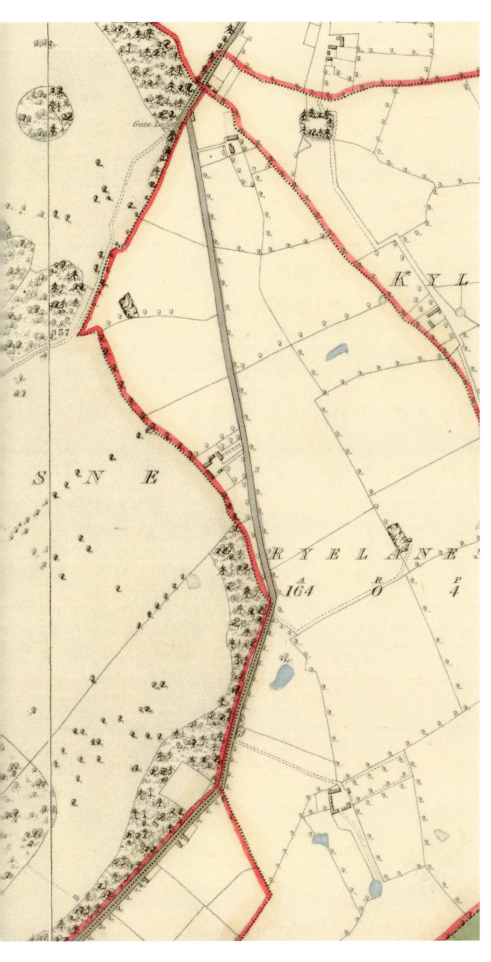

This Ordnance Survey map of 1842 (2nd ed.) shows the location of Desart Court (at center of the map) in County Kilkenny, Ireland. The land adjacent to the main buildings of Desart Court is known as "demesne"—an old Norman word for the land held and farmed by the landlord himself. Beyond the demesne were the areas leased to tenants, which were typically grouped into fields connected by walls, paths, or small roads. Desart Court was situated on an east-west orientation, with its farm buildings and walled gardens placed to the north, where they would not interrupt the pastoral vistas to the east, south, and west.

ABOVE *Few images exist to illustrate the interiors of Desert Court. This photograph from c. 1915 shows that the Entrance Hall was sumptuously decorated and hung with family portraits. From left to right are portraits of: Otway Cuffe, the second Earl of Desart by Thomas Clement Thompson; Colonel William Cuffe, younger brother of the second and third Barons, by Johan Zoffany; Catherine, Countess of Desart and wife of the second Earl, by Thomas Clement Thompson; and Maurice Nugent O'Connor of Mount Pleasant, King's County by his daughter Catherine.*

OPPOSITE *Two grand staircases were positioned at either end of the Desert Court. Elaborately carved oak scrollwork was used in place of balustrades under the staircase railings.*

OPPOSITE *The ceiling of the drawing room in Desart Court was elaborately decorated with rococo ornamentation that features busts and masks. The ornamentation was finished in cream against the white background.*

ABOVE *This view of Desart Court from its drive reveals the full scale of the Palladian mansion with its central block and two wings.*

IRISH INFLUENCES

Castle Inch and Castletown Cox

James Hoban would have been familiar with estates in the areas surrounding Kilkenny, Ireland, where he grew up, including Westpark, Callan House, Grange House, Castletown Cox, and, only 3 miles north of Desart Court, the Cuffe family's first great house, Castle Inch. The castle was built sometime after the Norman invasion of Ireland in the twelfth century and, along with its surrounding land, was awarded to Captain Joseph Cuffe for his service in Oliver Cromwell's army after the end of the siege of Kilkenny in 1650. The Cuffe family resided at Castle Inch until the construction of Desart Court in the 1730s. This 1842 Ordnance Survey map (opposite) shows the estate surrounding Castle Inch.

Located 18 miles south of Desart Court, the other major great house in the area was Castletown Cox. It was constructed in 1767 and is considered to be the apex of Irish country house design in the late eighteenth century. Designed by Davis Ducart for the untitled Cox family, the house is of similar scale to Desart Court, but the surrounding estate is smaller in keeping with the family's lesser social status.

100

Castletown Cox, constructed in 1767, was considered the apex of Irish country house design during last quarter of the eighteenth century. It is similar in scale and layout to Desart Court, with seven bays over a basement composition, a northeast-southwest orientation, and one-story wings surrounding a rectangular entrance courtyard.

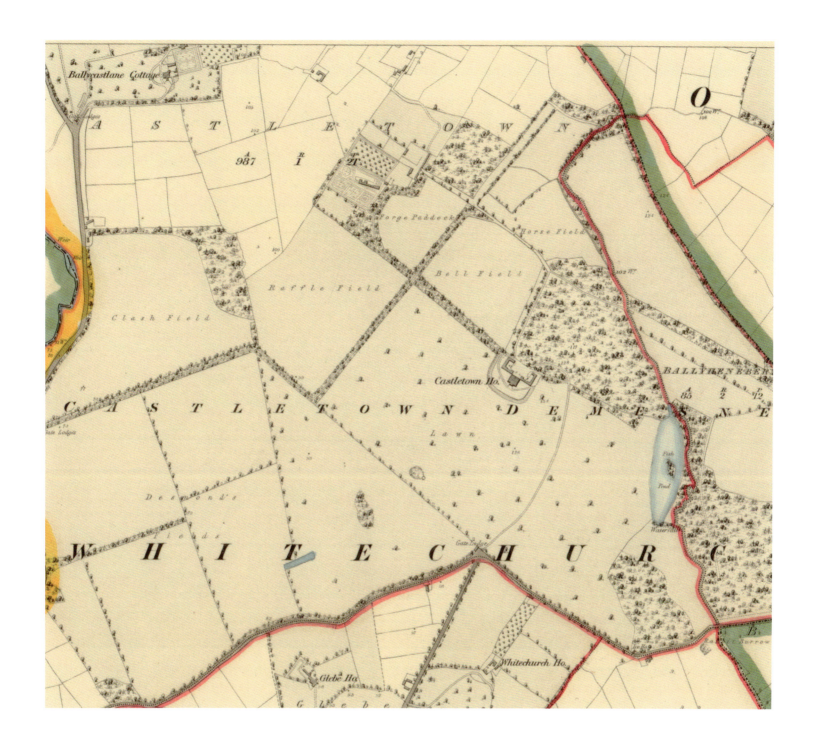

The demesne around Castletown Cox, as seen in this survey map made in 1842, was much smaller than that of Desart Court. It also lacked the vast wooded area typical of most country houses, including Desart Court, reflecting the family's lesser landholding and social status.

The Entrance Front of Castletown Cox features generous parkland lawns and a meandering drive.

IRISH INFLUENCES

Dublin

It is thought that James Hoban moved to Dublin during the mid-1770s with help from cousins who worked as stonemasons on the many construction sites in the city. The Dublin that Hoban encountered was in the midst of rapid change, with new, monumental buildings of the latest neoclassical style rising throughout the city.

Hoban likely found work as a carpenter on numerous building projects in the city. In a 1792 letter to the Commissioners, Hoban cited three buildings in Dublin that provided him with building experience on the scale of the President's House: the Royal Exchange, the Newcomen Bank, and the Custom House. These were among the largest projects in Dublin at the time.

Despite the new modern buildings, Dublin retained the urban form of its medieval city, as recorded in John Rocque's 1756 map. A year after the map's creation, the Wide Streets Commission was formed to radically rework the urban form of the city. The commission, well-versed in popular contemporary architecture and urban design of England and Continental Europe, became highly influential in the development of Dublin in the latter half of the eighteenth century. It would have also influenced general attitudes toward design in Dublin, including those in the Dublin Society School of Architectural Drawing, where Hoban enrolled likely by the late 1770s.

This view from Grafton Street looking into the College Green of Trinity College, Dublin, was painted in 1807 by Thomas Sautelle Roberts. The red brick building in the middle ground, to the left, is likely the Dublin Society School of Architectural Drawing where Hoban received his formal training as a designer of buildings. Hoban would have passed through the bustling College Green on his way to the school.

ABOVE *The Dublin Society School of Architectural Drawing was founded in 1764. This engraving of the school's Grafton Street home, where Hoban attended classes, was published in Walter Strickland's* Dictionary of Irish Artists *(1913) and reflects the simple building, clearly informed by neoclassical design.*

OPPOSITE *The study of geometry and perspective were central to the curriculum at the Dublin Society School of Architectural Drawing. Hoban and his fellow students would have studied plans and elevations of important structures and created their own designs according to specifications from their instructor. James Gibbs's* Rules for Drawing the Several Parts of Architecture *(1736), Sir William Chambers's* A Treatise on Civil Architecture *(1759. 2nd ed. 1768), and Andrea Palladio's* I Quattro Libri dell'Architettura *(1570) were the core texts assigned to the students. Patterns from Gibbs's* Book of Architecture *(1728) are seen in some of Hoban's later designs for finishes on the exterior of the President's House.*

A TREATISE ON Civil Architecture,

IN WHICH THE

Principles of that Art are laid down,

AND

Illustrated by a great Number of PLATES,

Accurately DESIGNED, and Elegantly ENGRAVED by the best HANDS.

By WILLIAM CHAMBERS,

Member of the IMPERIAL ACADEMY of ARTS in FLORENCE, of the ROYAL ACADEMY of ARCHITECTURE in PARIS, and of the SOCIETY of SCIENCES in STOCKHOLM, Architect to the KING, the QUEEN, and Her ROYAL HIGHNESS the Princess Dowager of WALES.

The SECOND EDITION.

LONDON:

Printed by J. DIXWELL, in St. Martin's Lane.

To be had at the Author's House in Berner Street, Oxford Road; likewise of CADELL, NOURSE, and WILSON, in the Strand; DURHAM, Charing Cross; R. DODSLEY in Pall-Mall; SAYER in Fleet Street; and WESLEY near Chancery Lane, Holborn.

M DCC LXVIII.

GEORGE R.

GEORGE the Second, by the Grace of God, King of Great-Britain, France and Ireland, Defender of the Faith, &c. To all to whom these Presents shall come, Greeting: WHEREAS *James Gibbs* of our City of *London*, hath humbly represented unto Us, that he hath with great Labour and Expence published a Work, intituled, *Rules for drawing the several parts of Architecture, in a more exact and easy manner than has been heretofore practised; by which all Fractions in dividing the principal Members and their Parts are avoided*; and hath humbly besought Us to grant him our Royal Privilege and Licence for the sole printing and publishing thereof, for the Term of Fourteen Years: We being willing to give all due Encouragement to Works of this nature, are graciously pleased to condescend to his Request. And We do therefore by these Presents, so far as may be agreeable to the Statute in that behalf made and provided, grant unto him the said *James Gibbs*, his Executors, Administrators, and Assigns, Our Licence for the sole printing and publishing the said Work, intituled, *Rules for drawing the several parts of Architecture, in a more exact and easy manner than has been heretofore practised; by which all Fractions, in dividing the principal Members and their Parts, are avoided*, for the Term of Fourteen Years, to be computed from the Date hereof; strictly forbidding all our Subjects within our Kingdoms and Dominions to reprint or abridge the same, either in the like or any other Volume or Volumes whatsoever, or to import, buy, vend, utter, or distribute any Copies thereof, reprinted beyond the Seas, during the aforesaid Term of Fourteen Years, without the Consent or Approbation of the said *James Gibbs*, his Heirs, Executors and Assigns, under their Hands and Seals first had and obtain'd, as they will answer the contrary at their Perils, whereof the Commissioners and other Officers of Our Customs, and the Master, Wardens and Company of *Stationers* are to take notice, that due Obedience be rendred to Our Pleasure herein declared.

Given at Our Court at St *James's* the nineteenth Day of *May* 1732. in the Fifth Year of Our Reign.

By his Majesty's Command,

HARRINGTON.

RULES FOR DRAWING

The several PARTS of

ARCHITECTURE,

IN A

More exact and easy manner than has been heretofore practised, by which all FRACTIONS, in dividing the principal MEMBERS and their Parts, are avoided.

By *JAMES GIBBS*.

The SECOND EDITION.

LONDON,

Printed by W. BOWYER for the AUTHOR.

MDCCXXXVI.

110

In November 1780, the Dublin Society awarded James Hoban this medal as a second place prize for "Drawings of Brackets, Stairs, Roofs &c." Given the choice of a medal or a substantial cash prize, Hoban chose the medal, rightly predicting it would benefit him throughout the course of his career. He did in fact use the medal as proof of his credentials while securing the commission to design and build the President's House. Cast in silver, the front side features Minerva holding a spear and cornucopia, leaning on a shield with an Irish harp. Around the image is the society's motto, "Nostri Plena Laboris," meaning "Our work bears fruit."

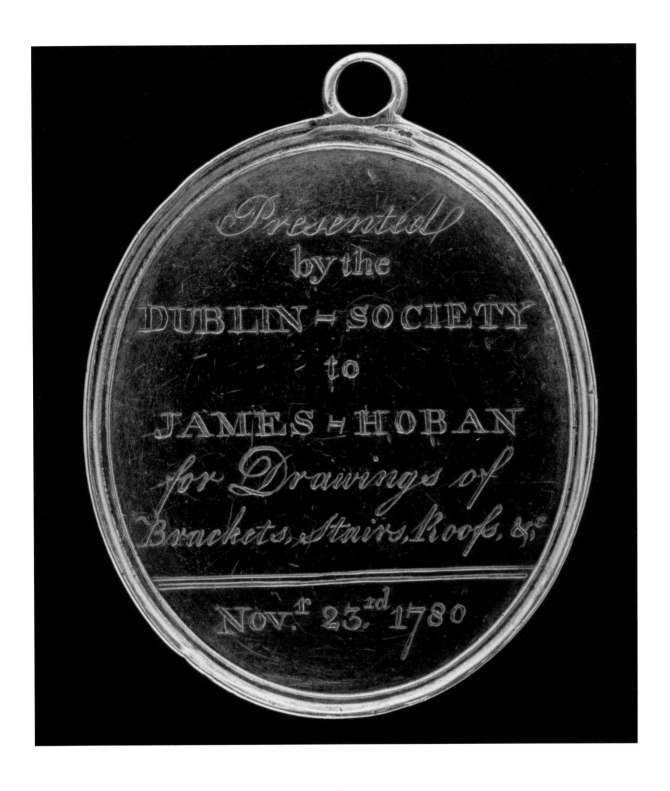

The reverse of Hoban's second place medal is inscribed, "Presented by the Dublin Society to James Hoban for Drawings of Brackets, Stairs, Roofs, &c, Nov. 23rd 1780." The medal is now in the collection of the Smithsonian Institution.

Thomas Ivory was the head of the Dublin Society School of Architectural Drawing from its founding in 1764 until his death in 1786. Ivory was an important influence on Hoban's development as a designer and builder. Hoban probably even worked as an apprentice with Ivory on several of his prominent building projects in Dublin, including Newcomen Bank. Attributed to John Trotter, this painting depicts Ivory (at center in brown) with his fellow Anglo-Irish architects in Dublin.

Gentlemen

Being universally acquainted with men in the Building line in Ireland, particularly with many able Stone Cutters in Dublin with whom I have been concerned in building, as the Royal Exchange, New Bank, and Custom House, all of which buildings were done in the same Stile as the business to be done here, and of nearly the same kind of Stone, to those men I would write if it meets the approbation of the Commissioners, to embark for this City, early in the Spring, and hold out such terms to them as the Commissioners may think proper, and would recommend to engage them for two Years, that the business may be done to a certainty; such hands have in Dublin a Guinea p.r Week, I would also recommend to encourage 4 or 6 compleat Brick layers, a pare of Sawyers fit for the purpose of the Building, and also a Smith of ability who will be much wanted here,

The Slate Quarry is a matter of much importance to this City and this building in particular, so hope the Commissioners will take such steps as will reduce the article of Slate to a Certainty, so as to know if the Slate on Potomak will ans.r the purpose, and also, the lime stone Quarry —

I had some conversation with M.r Reid a Stone cutter at Geo. Town, some time ago, to know on what terms he could furnish me 2000 feet of flaging of Potomak stone, to send to Chas.t.n; he said he believed he could furnish it to advantage by sawing it by hand, which leads me to conclude, if it can be found Practicable to use a mill, it woud ans.r many good purposes — Inclosed is a bill of the flooring plank with their necessary qualities, which if the commiss.rs

James Hoban began his two-page letter of November 1792 to the Commissioners for the District of Columbia by recommending that the Irish stonecutters with whom he became acquainted during his work on the Newcomen Bank, the Royal Exchange, and the Custom House in Dublin be hired for work on the President's House. He continued the letter by specifying supplies, including stone, nails, and lumber that would be needed for the project.

will please have an advertisement drawn, and include the Logs for Girders Joist Roofing &c. I will send it by the first post to Charlton, that there may be as speedy an ans.r as possible, the logs may be either white Oak, Yellow poplar, or Cypress, the last being equal to any for its Durability. I would wish that something may be done at this meeting respecting this article, as the Season for geting it is approaching fast

  Mr. Cabots information respecting the plank at 13 dollars p.r M is Reasonable, but it must be observed to him, they must be clear plank, what is understood by clear plank is, not three nots in a plank as large as a man can cover with his thumb, which is the Quality that I have described and expect to get, common he rates at 10 Doll.s p.r M

  With respect to the slate from Boston at 5 Doll.s p.r Sq.r it comes nearly to the price of Scotch Slate at Charlton, at five Guineas p.r M, one thousand of which has covered three squares, about £1..16..3 p.r Sq.r and the scotch slate has the advantage, by more than the difference in price, in the goodness of its Quality.

  Nails being constantly in demand here, I request the Commissioners will adopt some mode of geting a temporary supply, as what we have got is at an advanced price, and no regular method of being supplyed

  I would also wish, to have orders left, that if any Seasoned Stuff should come to Geo. Town, or coud be procured elsewhere to have it pur-

IRISH INFLUENCES

The Royal Exchange

The Royal Exchange was one of the buildings that Hoban said he worked on during his time in Dublin. Today's City Hall, the Exchange was the first large-scale neoclassical building in Ireland, and its construction marked a turning point in the architectural landscape of Dublin.

The Royal Exchange was commissioned by the Merchants' Guild of Dublin and designed by Thomas Cooley. Cooley, only 28 years old when he won the design competition, was from London, where he had apprenticed in the office of Robert Mylne. Constructed between 1769 and 1779, the Exchange was the first monumental building in Dublin to reflect archaeological neoclassicism. Essentially a square enclosing a circle, the latter being a columned rotunda, the Exchange occupied an acutely pitched site that ran from the walls of the old Dublin Castle to the bank of the River Liffey.

In 1852, the City Corporation of Dublin purchased the Royal Exchange building and converted it into City Hall. The open interior was subdivided to serve as office spaces, and twelve murals depicting events in Dublin's history were added to the dome. Between 1998 and 2000, Dublin City Council restored the building to its original 1779 state. It is still used by the Dublin City Council and contains the city archives.

The interior of the Royal Exchange is dominated by a rotunda (seen opposite) 46 feet in diameter ringed by columns and crowned by a dome, all in the richest materials. Inspired by the Pantheon, the rotunda follows Roman architecture more closely than such other contemporary neoclassical structures as Leinster House and Newcomen Bank.

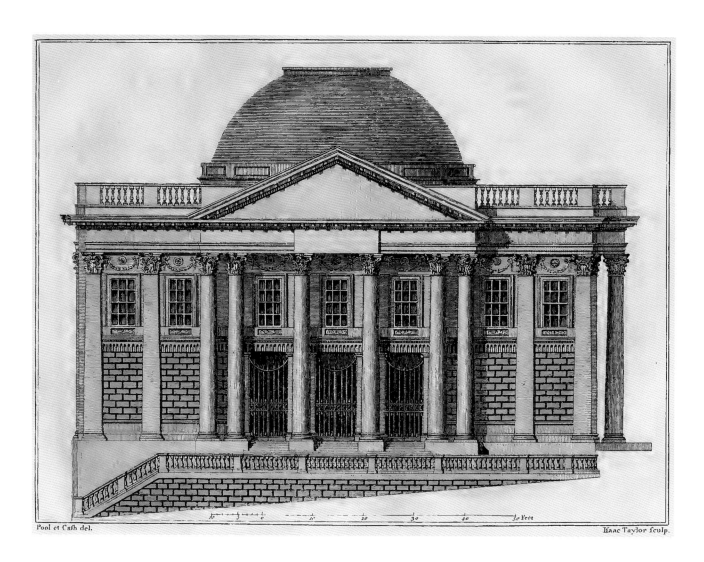

ABOVE *This engraving of the Royal Exchange was published in 1780 in* Views of the Most Remarkable Public Buildings, Monuments and Other Edifices in the City of Dublin *by Robert Pool and John Cash, a work undoubtedly familiar to James Hoban during his studies at the Dublin Society.*

OPPOSITE *Thomas Cooley's initial plan for the Royal Exchange called for the top of the rotunda dome to be left open, as it was in the Pantheon. But Ireland's rainy weather led to the decision to close the dome with an ornate stained glass window.*

The Royal Exchange, built entirely of Portland limestone, is situated across Castle Street from Newcomen Bank (seen at right in the photograph opposite). The massive Corinthian capitals were carved by Simon Vierpyl. The Exchange was a lively center of commercial transaction in eighteenth- and nineteenth-century Dublin. The large coffee house on the second floor next to corridors and open halls served offices and alcoves where brokers of all kinds dealt in wool, grain, and other products of a largely agricultural Ireland. It was also a gathering place for public meetings, and often for protests.

ABOVE AND OPPOSITE *Inside the Exchange two sets of elliptical stairs, built entirely of stone, dominate the two front corners of the building. The stairs are anchored into the limestone walls, leaving the space underneath open. In the bend of the stairs, Daniel O'Connell, Irish patriot and father of Irish nationalism, is honored with a statue commemorating his influential speech on the floor of the Exchange in protest of the Acts of Union of 1800 that dissolved the Irish Parliament.*

IRISH INFLUENCES

Newcomen Bank

In presenting his credentials to the Commissioners for the District of Columbia, James Hoban referenced his work on Newcomen Bank. The neoclassical structure was commissioned in 1778 by Sir William Gleadowe-Newcomen to serve as a bank and private residence. It was designed by Thomas Ivory and is considered his finest work. It is possible that Hoban, as a student in the School of Architectural Drawing, worked as an apprentice to Ivory and thus would have had a role in the construction of the bank.

Newcomen Bank was designed to be both city apartment and office, an idea stylish in cities in Europe at the time, with the business rooms below and elegant residences above. The interior consisted of three oval rooms on the main or ground floor, devised by Ivory to create rational spaces within the odd, trapezoid shape the building had taken to accommodate the triangular lot. One was a drawing room, where Sir William received and sometimes dined with upper-class clients, while the other two were working areas of the bank. These ovals rooms are likely predecessors of the oval rooms designed for the President's House by Hoban.

In 1862, the Hibernian Bank, which had previously bought the building from the Newcomen descendants, engaged the architect William Caldbeck to double the size of the building. The added section was to face the newly created Lord Edward Street and exactly mirror the old, with the two parts united by a columned porch. Today Newcomen Bank serves as a government tax office and is one of Dublin's finest examples of late eighteenth-century neoclassicism.

This view of Newcomen Bank captures the eighteenth-century half of the building on the left, with the added section duplicating the facade on the right, and reflects the building's original width.

Newcomen Bank is seen on the right in this engraving made in 1788. During the redesign of Dublin, Castle Street became a banking quarter centered around the Royal Exchange. Newcomen Bank occupied a strategic location in the new quarter opposite both the Royal Exchange and the entrance to Dublin Castle.

The fine decorative carvings on the facade of Newcomen Bank were executed by Simon Vierpyl, an acclaimed sculptor and stonemason of Dutch origins. Vierpyl spent several years in Rome creating copies of classical sculptures for tourists on their "Grand Tours." He arrived in Dublin in 1756, hired to supervise construction on the Casino at Marino. He then went on to create decorative carvings on several prominent buildings in the city including Newcomen Bank and the Royal Exchange. Hoban would have been familiar with Vierpyl through his own work on Newcomen Bank and the Royal Exchange.

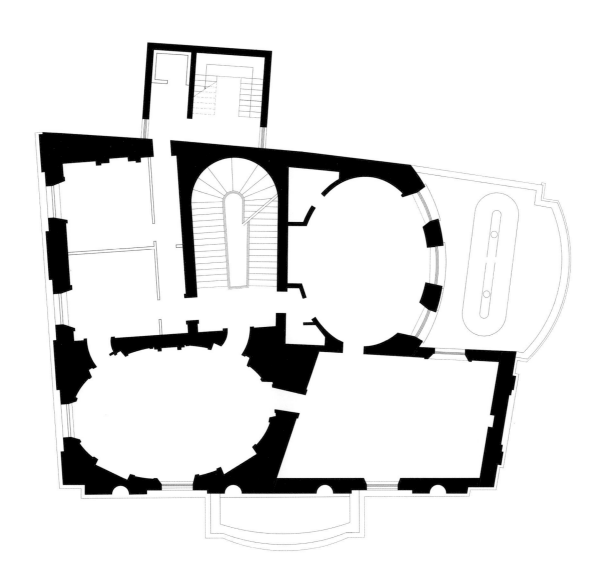

This modern diagram illustrates the first floor plan of Newcomen Bank, which features oval-shaped rooms designed by Thomas Ivory to create an overall shape that fit the irregular shape of the building plot. The oval room at the front was likely used by Newcomen as the main bank parlor, where he welcomed clients.

ABOVE *Limestone from the Isle of Portland in Dorset, England, was used to build many prominent neoclassical buildings in Ireland, including both Newcomen Bank and the Royal Exchange in Dublin. Limestone has been quarried in this area since Roman times.*

OPPOSITE *The Portland limestone walls of Newcomen Bank are rusticated externally on the public (or ground) level and smooth-faced above on the residential floors. The rustication is similar to Hoban's treatment of the Ground Floor level of the White House.*

ABOVE *In his design of Newcomen Bank, Ivory carefully situated the first floor oval room, the most prominent room on the banking floor, to have views of both the Royal Exchange and the entrance to Dublin Castle. The walls of the room feature arcades that incorporate doors, windows, and storage recesses.*

OPPOSITE *The centerpiece of the first floor oval room is the trompe l'oeil ceiling painting attributed to the Italian painter Vincent Waldré, also known as Vincenzo Valdrè. The scene depicts cherubs bearing flowers and wreaths against the backdrop of a clouded sky. Waldré is also credited with painting the ceilings in St. Patrick's Hall in Dublin Castle, considered the most significant painted ceiling in Ireland.*

Ornate neoclassical plasterwork is seen throughout the decorative spaces in Newcomen Bank, including on the joinery in the oval parlor. Here in the pediment is an alternating pattern of two styles of classical candelabrum based on ancient Roman forms connected by stylized swags.

Part of Ivory's plan for Newcomen Bank included a central top-lit open-well stair hall. The ceiling of the stair hall is ornamented with delicate plasterwork featuring typical neoclassical forms such as griffins, swags, scrolling acanthus, and medallions. This plasterwork is similar to the work of Charles Thorp on the Royal Exchange.

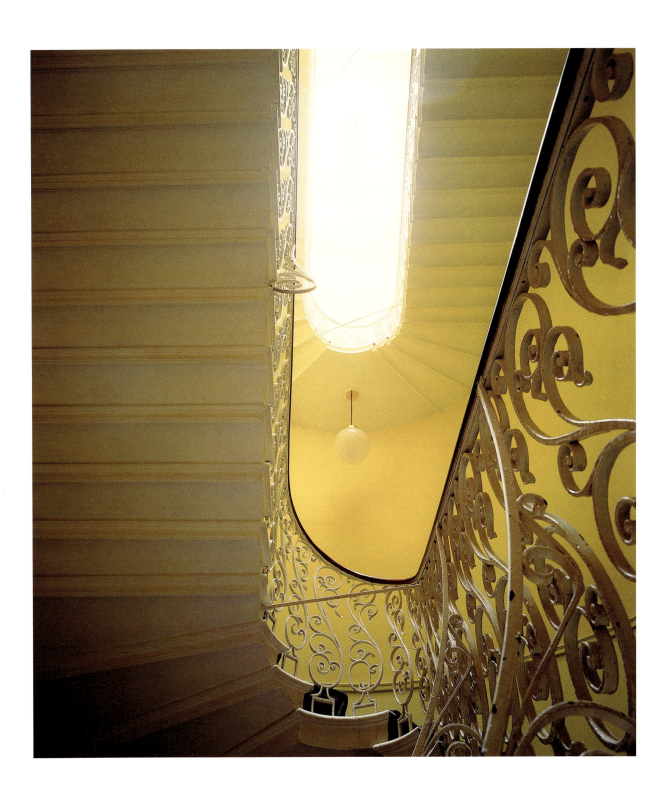

The other commanding feature of the bank's interior is the monumental grand stair of stone that dominates the elegant central hall. The thin limestone treads are mortised into the stone walls, and the fine wrought-iron railing curves two stories up to a domed skylight decorated with classical designs in stucco.

The Royal Exchange and Newcomen Bank, at the left and right respectively, flank Castle Street leading to Dublin Castle Gate in this early nineteenth-century view by Henry Brocas.

IRISH INFLUENCES

The Custom House

The Custom House, designed by James Gandon and completed between 1781 and 1791, was another of the monumental buildings in Dublin that Hoban claimed to have worked on. Gandon's Custom House, located on the northeastern quays of the River Liffey, replaced the city's old Custom House that sat on the quays near Dublin Castle and the Royal Exchange in the heart of the historic city. The location of the new Custom House was part of the ongoing redevelopment and expansion of Dublin in the latter half of the eighteenth century. Gandon's Custom House is considered to be a masterpiece of European neoclassicism. In 1792, the artist James Malton captured the finished building in this engraving.

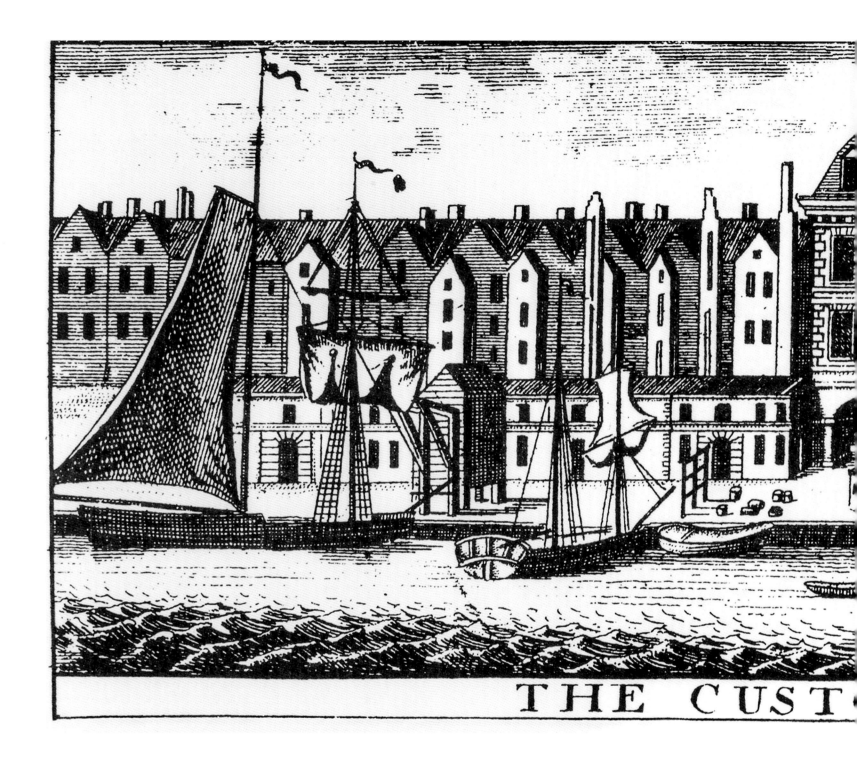

The first Dublin Custom House was designed by Thomas Burgh and completed in 1707. It sat on the south bank of the River Liffey, a location that facilitated the unloading of ships. In this engraving published in 1728, Charles Brooking shows three ships berthed at the Custom House Quay as several smaller boats await to bring the goods farther upriver. By the end of the century, the building had been replaced by Gandon's grand Custom House.

M HOUSE

IRISH INFLUENCES

Leinster House

Leinster House, or Kildare House as it was first known, was built for the Earl of Kildare in the country outside Dublin. Warned that he was building too far out of the city, the earl declared that society would follow him, and it did over the years, bringing a whole townscape of fine buildings that diminished the original impact of the building as a country house. Designed by German-born architect Richard Castle (or Cassels), the house was built starting in 1745 and was completed about 1750. Castle was Ireland's leading architect at the time working in the Palladian style. It was this prominent country house that served as the chief inspiration for James Hoban in his design for the President's House.

The house was renamed in 1766 when the earl became the Duke of Leinster—Leinster being the name of the province in which Dublin stands. In 1818, the family sold Leinster House to the Dublin Society for use as its headquarters and relocated permanently to Carton, their country house in Maynooth, County Kildare, also designed by Richard Castle. In 1924, the Irish Free State purchased the house for parliamentary use and today it is the home of the two houses of the Oireachtas, the National Parliament.

Hoban's descriptions of Leinster House undoubtedly convinced George Washington that it was a worthy model for the President's House. Hoban knew the house well, possibly even observing the work of remodeling the ground floor dining room of the house while a student under Thomas Ivory. It was commonly said even in the early days of the President's House that Leinster House was the model, something Hoban seems to have made well known. Like the exterior, the plans of the two houses are similar enough to further suggest the relationship.

The West Front view of Leinster House is seen here in a 1792 engraving by James Malton. Castle's design situated the West Front to face the city, drawing from the tradition of the French hotel. Hoban laid out the President's House in a similar manner, with the North Front along the central Pennsylvania Avenue and the South Front facing the verdant areas of the gardens and Tiber Creek where it flowed into the Potomac River.

ABOVE *Made in 1750, this survey includes Leinster House (labeled Kildare House) in the lower left corner and the landscape between it and the sea.*

OPPOSITE *William Robert FitzGerald, second Duke of Leinster, was a notable patron of the Dublin Society when Hoban was enrolled in its Architectural Drawing School. The duke's brother, Lord Edward FitzGerald, became a symbolic leader for the United Irishmen during the 1790s in efforts to achieve an independent Ireland. Lord Edward, as he was commonly known, became a convert to the ideas of liberty and equality while living in Paris after fighting for the British in the American Revolution. He became known throughout Ireland, and America, as the leading popular supporter of the United Irishmen.*

148

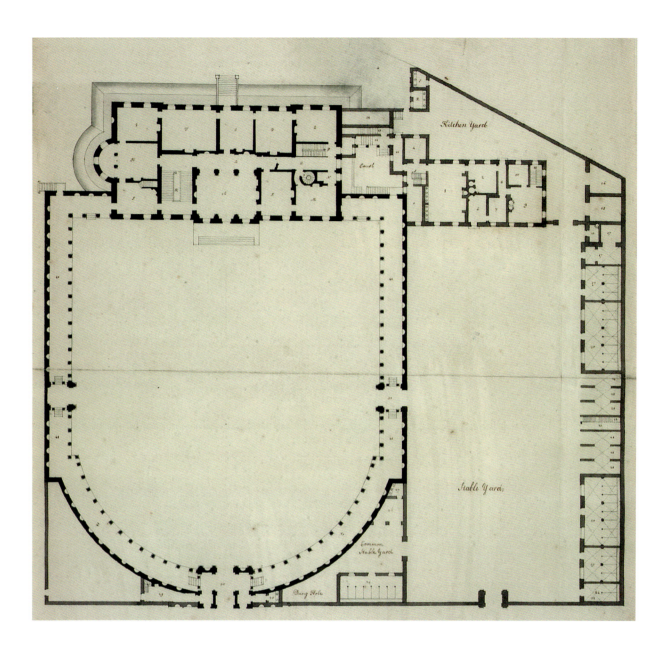

OPPOSITE *The East Front of Leinster House, drawn by Thomas Cunningham in 1790 (top) and photographed in 2007 (bottom), was designed to serve as the garden front from which residents could enjoy vistas of Dublin Bay and the fields of Ballsbridge and Baggots Rath to the east. Hoban, familiar with the dual character of the two fronts at Leinster House, situated the President's House in a similar manner.*

ABOVE *Richard Castle's plan for Leinster House, c. 1745, shows how carefully he situated the house, service buildings, and gardens to exploit the site's interstitial, suburban character. He designed Leinster House to be both town house and country house.*

II

The Builder in America

WHILE THE EXACT DATE of Hoban's arrival in America is unknown, it is believed that he set sail for America soon after he completed his training at the Dublin Society School of Architectural Drawing. Possibly enticed by the young nation's wealth of building projects, he first settled in Philadelphia. Hoban's first documented appearance in America is a notice he placed in both Charleston and Philadelphia newspapers in May 1785 advertising his carpentry services. Finding the Philadelphia building trade crowded and lacking connections in the city, he soon moved south to Charleston to work with a distant relation, Pierce Purcell.

In Charleston, Hoban soon found success and quickly established himself within the fabric of the city. The connections he made in Charleston eventually paved his path to meeting President George Washington and receiving the commission to build the President's House.

Hoban is seen here in his only known portrait made from life, likely in his 40s. The small wax bas-relief is attributed to the German-born artist John Christian Rauschner, c. 1800, and is in the White House collection.

THE BUILDER IN AMERICA

Charleston, South Carolina

Upon moving to Charleston, James Hoban lived with Pierce Purcell and his family at 43 Trott Street in the Ansonborough section of the old city. Purcell was probably a relation who had emigrated from Ireland years before. Hoban soon built his own home next door, which he occupied or rented until he sold the property in 1798. Hoban and Purcell formed a lucrative partnership. Their most notable documentable project was the Charleston Theater. It is also believed that the pair was responsible for rebuilding the Charleston State House, which had burned in 1788.

Beyond their building projects, Purcell and Hoban established themselves in Charleston society as founding members of both St. Mary's Roman Catholic Church and the Masonic Lodge of Charleston. It was through his work and these groups that Hoban made important connections with Charleston's most prominent citizens. When President George Washington visited the city during a tour of the southern states in the spring of 1791, Hoban's connections proved invaluable. Hoban's fortuitous introduction to the president was orchestrated by General William Moultrie, Jacob Read, and, in particular, Henry Laurens. Laurens, a good friend of Washington, became acquainted with Hoban during the rebuilding of the Charleston State House, later renamed the Charleston County Courthouse, of which Laurens was the principal patron. The prominent statesman from Charleston is seen in this portrait painted in 1781 while he was held in the Tower of London during the American Revolution.

Circumstances suggest that Hoban and his Charleston partner Pierce Purcell rebuilt the burned out Charleston State House in 1790. Their building, which soon became the Charleston County Courthouse when the South Carolina capital moved to Columbia, holds a striking resemblance to Leinster House in Dublin. Completed around the time of George Washington's visit to Charleston, it is possible that this structure impressed Hoban's abilities upon Washington. The courthouse is seen in this photograph, c. 1880.

> # Architecture.
>
> SEVERAL applications being made to the subscriber, has induced him to establish an EVENING SCHOOL, for the instruction of young men in Architecture, to commence the 3d May next. From the experience he has had and the testimonial approbation of one of the first academies of arts and sciences in Europe, he hopes to merit the sanction of the public, and give satisfaction to his employers. Terms and hours of attendance will be made known at No. 43, Trott-street.
>
> James Hoban.
>
> ☞ He refers to the following gentlemen for his abilities, viz.
>
> Thomas Gadsden, George A. Hall, Roger Smith, Daniel Cannon, Esquires.
>
> Plans, elevations, sections of buildings, &c. drawn at a short notice, and the different branches of carpentery executed on the lowest terms and most approved manner, by
>
> Hoban & Purcell.
>
> April 17.   5t w

ABOVE *In 1790, Hoban & Purcell established their own school of architectural drawing, modeled after the Dublin Society School, in their shared home and office on Trott Street. They advertised the school in the* Charleston City Gazette *on April 17, 1790.*

OPPOSITE *On August 9, 1792, the* Charleston City Gazette *announced that Hoban had won the design competition for the President's House and asserted Charleston's pride in its former resident. The article details Hoban's success at the Dublin Society Architectural Drawing School and his projects in Charleston. It also references Hoban's meeting with George Washington while the president was visiting the city.*

From a Correspondent.

We have received accounts from the northward, and with much satisfaction, that Mr. *James Hoban*, of this city, has furnished the best plan, section and elevation for the presidental palace in the federal city of Washington. It is also expected that his plan for a capitol will be preferred.—On this occasion we think it but justice to observe, that Mr. Hoban, as a man of abilities, is unassuming and diffident. When a mere boy, he received a mark of distinction from the royal society of Dublin, which none else could then atchieve. We wish him success, and every encouragement the city of Washington can afford.—Mr. Hoban furnished a plan, or was about to do it here, for an orphan-house, but whether adopted or not we will not pretend to assert: certain it is, that he relinquished furnishing his plan, &c. unless he was permitted to work it up himself.—When the President of the United States honored this city with a visit last year, Mr. Hoban was introduced to him, as a man of merit and of genius, under the patronage of general Moultrie, Mr. Butler, &c. And we may safely add, that it is no small matter of universal satisfaction to the citizens of Carolina, that their fellow-citizen, Hoban, has succeeded in this enterprize.

158

In the spring of 1791, while President George Washington visited Charleston as part of his southern tour, the city rented to him and his entourage this three-story mansion providing the president privacy during his stay. It was likely at this house that James Hoban was introduced to the president. Washington later remembered the meeting and those who facilitated the introduction; however, he did not recall Hoban's name. Known today as the Heyward-Washington House, the site commemorates Washington's stay in Charleston.

After their initial introduction in Charleston, Hoban met with President Washington again in June 1792 at the President's House in Philadelphia. It was here that Hoban presented his references and credentials to the president, initiating his role as the builder of the President's House. The house in Philadelphia was located at Sixth and Market Streets, one block north of Independence Hall, and is seen here in an engraving by William L. Beton, c. 1830.

THE BUILDER IN AMERICA

The Federal City of Washington

In June 1792 James Hoban traveled to the Federal City to survey the site of the President's House. It was then that Hoban presented the Commissioners of the District of Columbia a letter of introduction and recommendation from President George Washington. Hoban would establish a home for himself in the city he helped to build, and he remained there for the rest of his life.

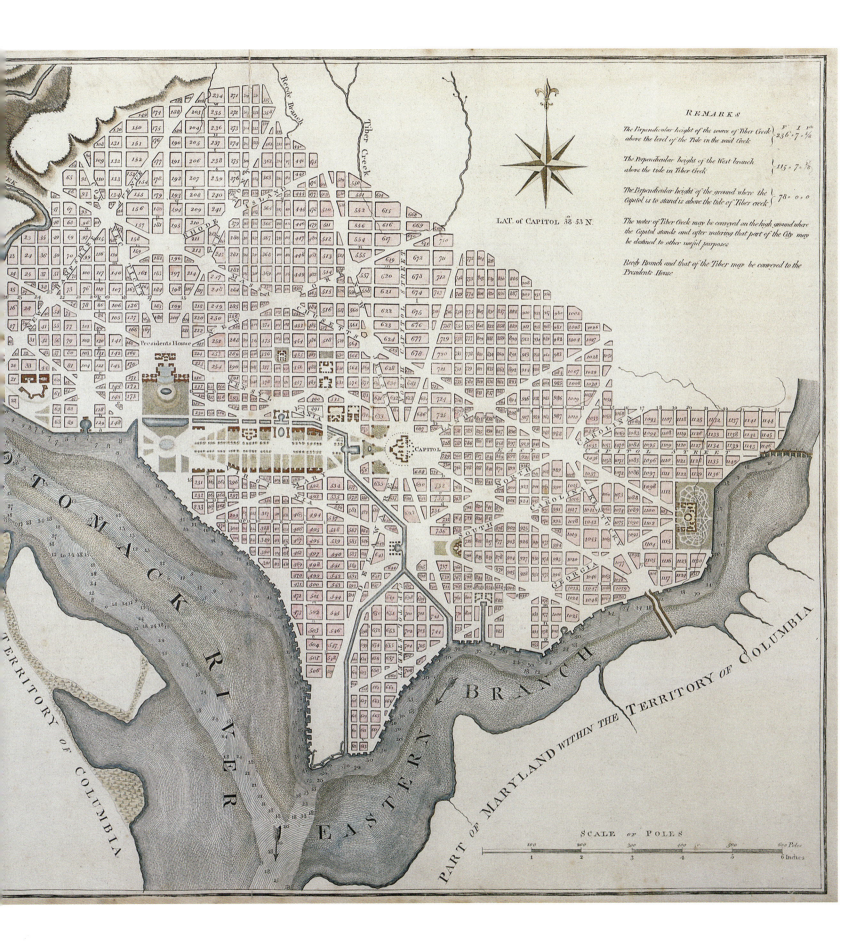

162

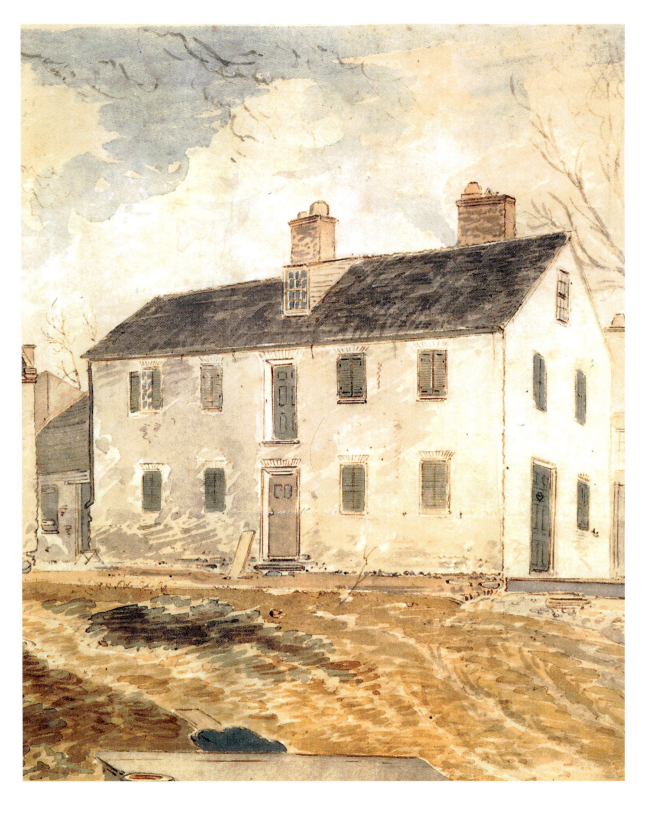

Hoban's residence in the Federal City was located on the north side of F Street between Fourteenth and Fifteenth Streets, just to the east of Rhodes Tavern. This watercolor by James Madison Alden, painted from the rear of the house on a wintry day in 1874, captured its appearance a few years before it was razed in 1880.

At the center of Hoban's F Street neighborhood was Rhodes Tavern, the oldest commercial building in downtown Washington, which served as an unofficial city hall. Most of the meetings Hoban attended relating to militia, political, civic, and charitable organizations were conducted here. This watercolor of the corner of F Street and Fifteenth Street by Anne-Marguerite Hyde de Neuville, depicts the building that originally housed the tavern before it became the Bank of Metropolis, as seen here in 1817.

James Hoban married Susana Sewall at Holy Trinity Church in Georgetown on January 13, 1799. Their marriage is recorded with the third of four entries on this page of the church marriage registry (above). The entry includes witnesses Clement Sewall, Susana's father, and Edward and Joseph Neale, cousins of the bride on her mother's side. James and Susana had ten children together during their twenty-three years of marriage. Holy Trinity Church (opposite) was used for worship until a new, larger church was constructed in 1851. The original church was renamed the Chapel of St. Ignatius and is still used by Holy Trinity Parish for smaller ecclesiastical celebrations.

THE BUILDER IN AMERICA

The President's House

By the fall of 1793, Hoban had redrawn his initial design for the President's House with alterations dictated by President Washington. Washington had placed Hoban in charge of the entire project, with all departments of building—carpentry, stonemasonry, and brickwork—under his supervision. Although Washington would never live in the house, he drove the stakes for the foundation himself and visited the building site as the walls rose. With his illustration, *Building the First White House*, made in c. 1931 for the Pennsylvania Railroad (opposite), the artist N. C. Wyeth imagined Washington and Hoban surveying the scene at the construction site.

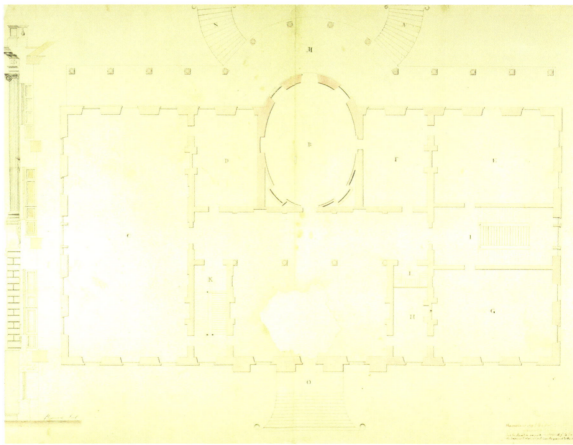

James Hoban's final design for the North Front of the President's House (top), made in the autumn of 1793, was modified from his original proposal by President Washington and the commissioners to increase the volume of the house by 20 percent and reduce the height from three to two stories over a ground-level basement. The resemblance to the North Front of Leinster House (opposite top) is clearly seen in the pediment and window hoods, attached Ionic columns, smooth ashlar walls, and broad pediment over the central columned section. The plan of the State Floor (bottom) is probably Hoban's first competition drawing made in summer 1792 and reflects the influence of the floor plan of Leinster House (opposite bottom). The most notable difference is Hoban's addition of the oval-shaped room on the south side of the house. Hoban's original section for the North Front of the White House, drawn at the left of the floor plan, bears reference to the facade of Desart Court (pages 88, 97).

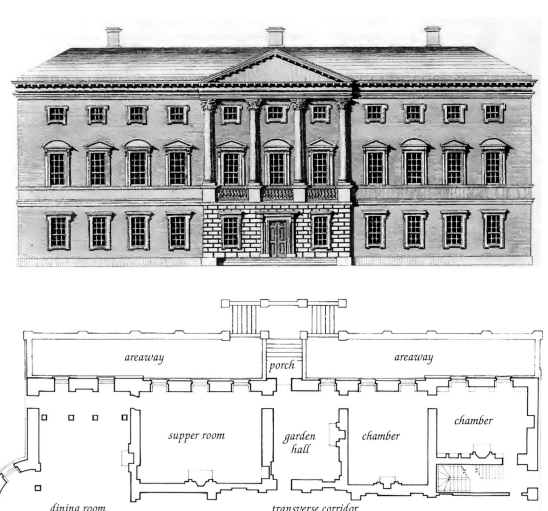

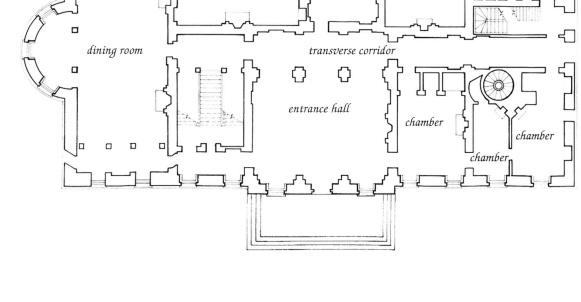

This view of the West, or Principal, Front of Leinster House (top) appeared in Views of the Most Remarkable Public Buildings, Monuments and Other Edifices in the City of Dublin, *published in 1780, and likely served as reference for Hoban when creating his north elevation for the President's House. The modern rendering of the floor plan of Leinster House (bottom) shows an arrangement of rooms, stairs, other details similar to that drawn by Hoban for the President's House.*

With his 2007 painting, Building the President's House, *Peter Waddell imagined the scene at the construction site in 1796. In the foreground is James Hoban between commissioner William Thornton and his carpenter and partner Pierce Purcell, standing on the high east wall, looking down into what would be the East Room. On the right are enslaved carpenters. Stonemasons build the outer walls of dressed sandstone, while brickmasons line them for support with soft clay bricks. The workers' village, brick kiln, and Potomac River are seen in the distance.*

THE BUILDER IN AMERICA

The Catholic Church

Soon after his arrival in Washington in 1792, James Hoban became a part of a group of influential Catholic men who helped establish the first churches in the city to serve the men—some with their families—coming to the new Federal City to work on the various building projects.

In 1794 Hoban helped found the first church of any denomination in the Federal City, St. Patrick's Church, and he stayed committed to it in the coming decades, constructing a new church building in 1809 and later expanding it and adding the Washington Catholic Seminary building in 1815. Near Capitol Hill, Hoban built St. Mary's Chapel in 1806, and in 1820 he contributed to the founding of the second Catholic church in the city, St. Peter's Church. In 1806, soon after completing his major work on the President's House, Hoban was employed by his friend and fellow prominent Catholic, James Barry, to design a chapel on Barry's estate for the use of the surrounding community. While the chapel was demolished soon after 1819, the cornerstone (opposite) was saved and is now in an outer wall of the Holy Name Chapel at St. Dominic's Church in Southwest Washington, D.C. The inscription reads, "In the name of the blessed undivided Trinity. Amen. This first stone of a small Roman Catholic Church is laid in the city of Washington in the year of our Lord & Saviour Jesus Christ 1806, and dedicated to the blessed Virgin Mary under title & name of Saint Mary's GLORIA IN EXCEL DEO. Erected by & at the charge of James Barry."

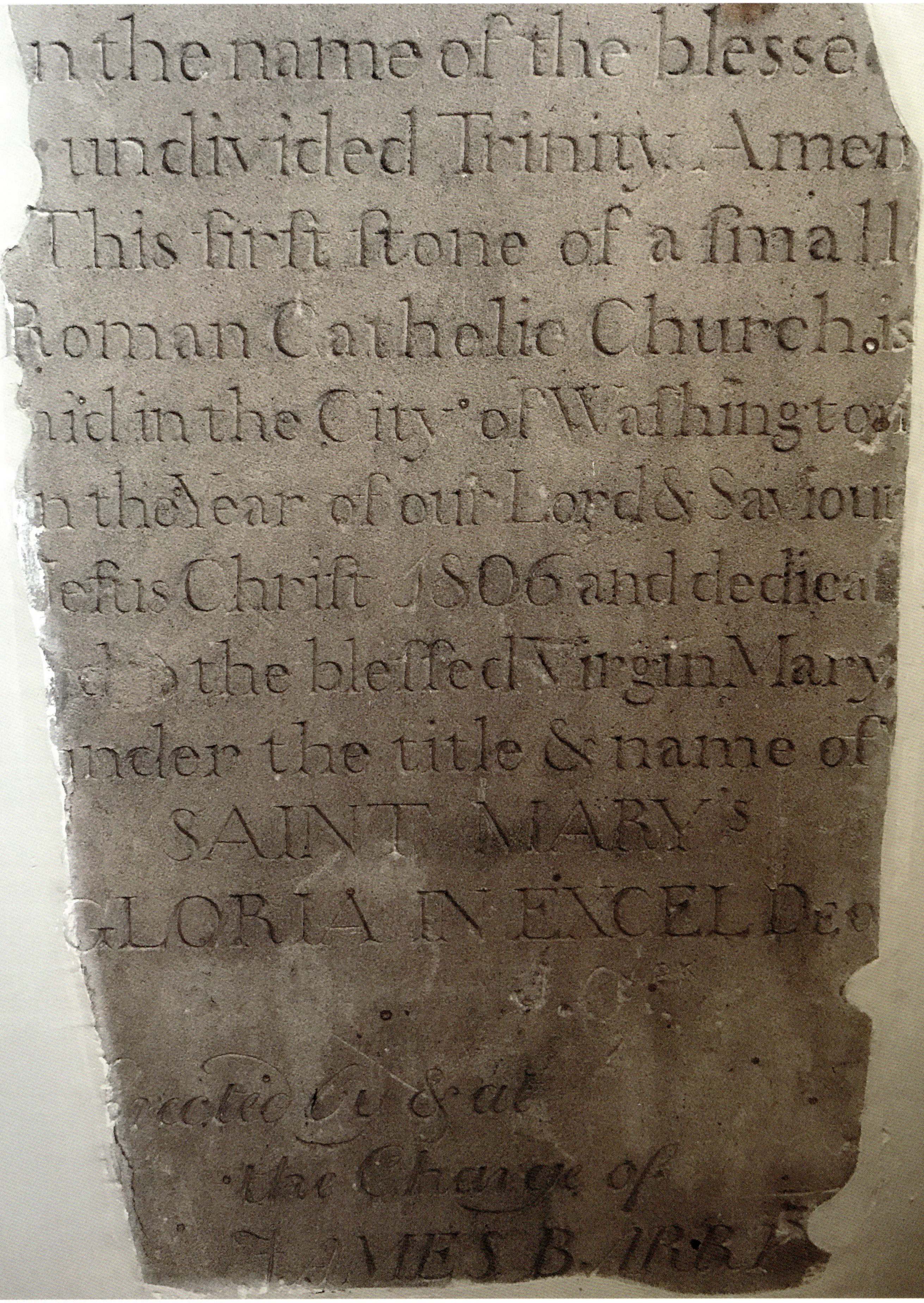

n the name of the blessed
undivided Trinity. Amen
This first stone of a small
Roman Catholic Church is
laid in the City of Washington
in the Year of our Lord & Saviour
Jesus Christ 1806 and dedicated
to the blessed Virgin Mary,
under the title & name of
SAINT MARY's
GLORIA IN EXCEL Deo

Erected by & at
the Charge of
JAMES BARRY

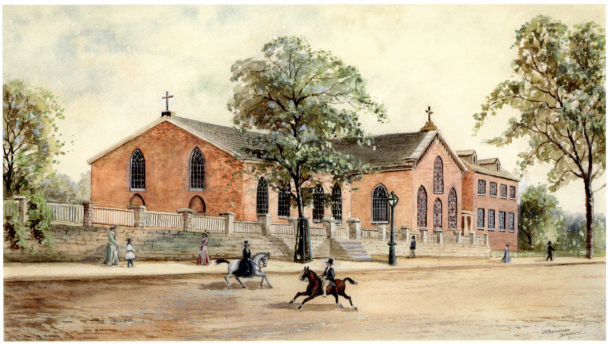

These watercolors of St. Patrick's Catholic Church by J. H. Bockelman are the earliest images of the church and school that James Hoban designed and built. The first view (top) likely depicts the church between 1809 and 1814, after the parish's second church was built and before the school was added. The second (bottom), made c. 1830, includes the 1815 addition that added the Washington Catholic Seminary to the structure. St. Patrick's was laid out in the shape of a cross, a traditional shape for Catholic churches, and closely resembles the lines and shape of St. Mary's Church in Callan, County Kilkenny, Ireland (opposite), which James Hoban would have known in his youth. Constructed in 1460, St. Mary's was a major landmark in the market town of Callan.

176

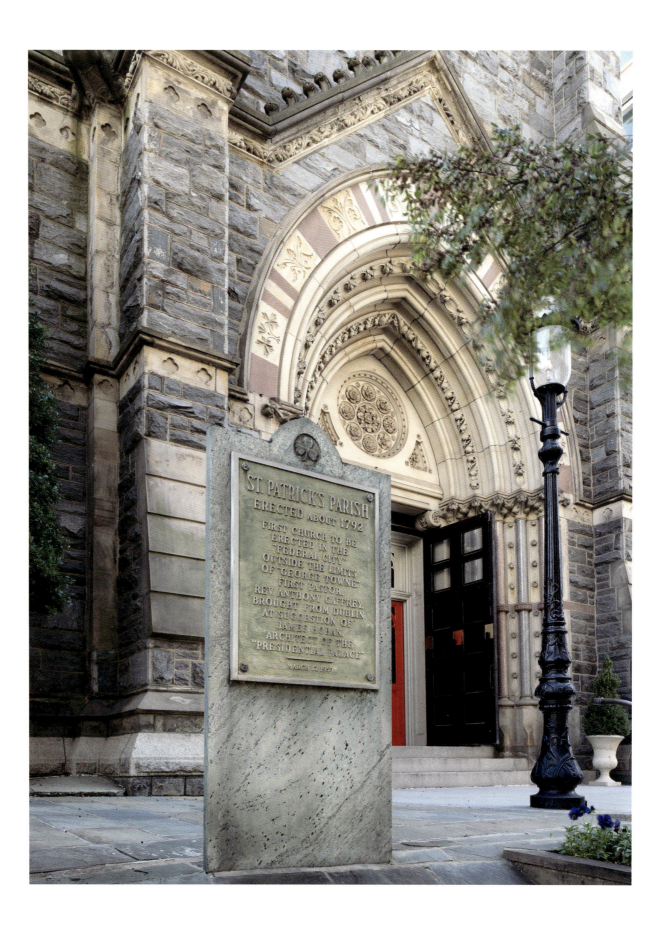

St. Patrick's is the oldest Catholic parish in the Federal City of Washington, D.C. James Hoban is remembered with a plaque outside the current structure, which was completed in 1884.

THE BUILDER IN AMERICA

The Freemasons

James Hoban was active in the Freemasons during his early years in the City of Washington, having transferred his membership in the Masonic order from Charleston, South Carolina, to Federal Lodge No. 8 in Georgetown. On October 13, 1792, Hoban participated in a full Masonic ceremony to lay the cornerstone for the President's House. The cornerstone was laid atop a polished brass plate inscribed with the names of the president, the commissioners, James Hoban, and Collen Williamson, master mason. President Washington was not present at the event that included a procession, an oration, and a feast. The banker's marks of more than forty stonemasons have been found carved into the back or hidden surfaces of the building stones at the President's House. These marks are the signatures of masons who worked on the house during the 1790s, after the 1814 fire, and during the addition of the North and South Porticoes in the 1820s.

The following year, Hoban played an important role in founding Freemason Lodge No. 15 of Maryland, which is still in operation today as Federal Lodge No. 1 under the Grand Lodge of Washington, D.C. It was to be the first lodge that met regularly in the City of Washington, and its first members were primarily workmen involved in the building of the United States Capitol. The charter, issued September 12, 1793, designated James Hoban as Worshipful Master. Just six days later, on September 18, 1793, Hoban attended the laying of the cornerstone of the United States Capitol in his role as Worshipful Master of the new Federal Lodge that he helped to establish.

ABOVE: *On September 18, 1793, James Hoban attended the laying of the cornerstone of the United States Capitol in his role as Worshipful Master of the new Federal Lodge that he helped to establish. Depicted above by Allyn Cox in 1958, the stone was laid in a masonic ceremony led by President George Washington (center in full Masonic regalia) and attended by Hoban (seen on the far left holding a floor plan) and members of his newly established lodge as well as government and military officials and private citizens.*

LEFT: *The masons whose labor built the walls of the President's House are remembered by their marks, carved into the stones of the house.*

THE BUILDER IN AMERICA

Slavery

James Hoban became a slave owner sometime after he established himself in Charleston, South Carolina. According to a 1789 advertisement in the *City Gazette*, Hoban sought the return of his enslaved worker Peter, who was described as a carpenter. Along with the names of three other enslaved craftsmen, the name Peter is seen again on a May 1795 carpenters' payroll for the President's House. These four men were just a few of the enslaved workers on the project.

Hoban not only utilized enslaved labor on his building sites but he appears to have also sold enslaved persons, as evidenced by a February 1805 advertisement (opposite top) in the *National Intelligencer*. It is not known whether Hoban owned the woman and her three children listed for sale in the advertisement, or if he was selling the enslaved people on behalf of someone else.

The 1820 census (opposite bottom) reveals that James Hoban (seventh from bottom) had nine enslaved individuals in his household at the time.

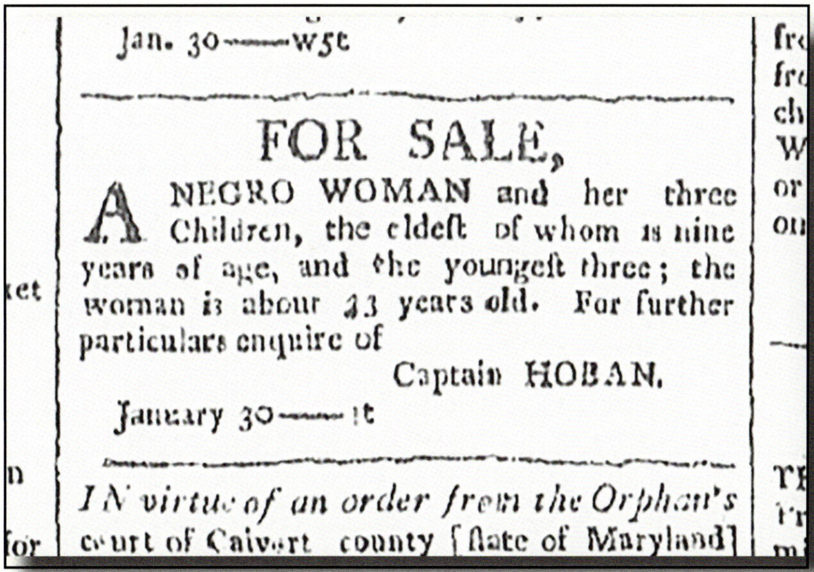

Jan. 30—w5t

FOR SALE,

A NEGRO WOMAN and her three Children, the eldest of whom is nine years of age, and the youngest three; the woman is about 33 years old. For further particulars enquire of

Captain HOBAN.

January 30—1t

IN virtue of an order from the Orphan's court of Calvert county [state of Maryland]

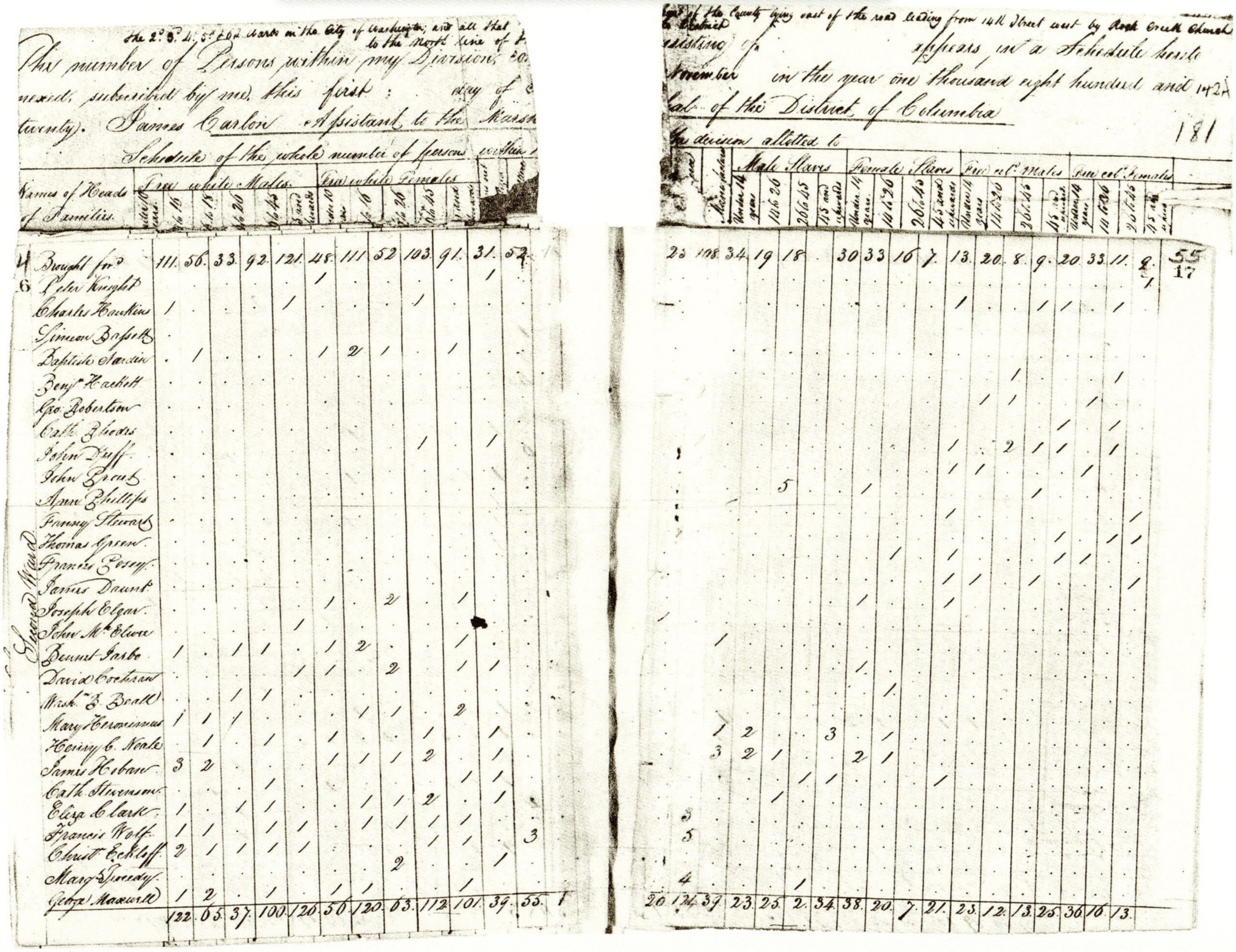

While the 1820 census lists nine enslaved persons as part of James Hoban's household, only two enslaved persons and one free woman of color are listed in his household in the 1830 census. It is possible that as he grew older, he no longer needed a large enslaved workforce in his home. However, an advertisement in the National Intelligencer *on April 7, 1832, indicates that Hoban may have owned eight enslaved persons at the time of his death. The Hoban household is recorded in the second entry on this page of the 1830 census.*

John Sepford by the Marshal of the District (or Territory) of _Columbia_

SLAVES												FREE COLORED PERSONS												TOTAL
MALES						FEMALES						MALES						FEMALES						
Under 10	10 to 24	24 to 36	36 to 55	55 to 100	100, &c.	under 10	10 to 24	24 to 36	36 to 55	55 to 100	100, &c.	under 10	10 to 24	24 to 36	36 to 55	55 to 100	100, &c.	under 10	10 to 24	24 to 36	36 to 55	55 to 100	100, &c.	
	1						1												1					2
							1																	9
												1												9
													1	1					1					3
																								18
																								3
	3	1				2		2																13
																1	1							1
													1						1					2
															1						1			2
													1						2					3
1	1						1																	8
1																								6
																								3
																								6
						1	1																	8
												1	1			1	3	1						7
																			1					7
																								4
												1								1	1			3
																								2
																								3
							1					2							1					11
1		1					1	1	1															7
1																				1				4
																								5
						2																		8
8	2	1		1		9	1	3	1			2	7	2	2	1		1	13	3	3	1		161

THE BUILDER IN AMERICA

Return to the President's House

On November 1, 1800, President John Adams moved into the President's House. Throughout the next fourteen years, Hoban periodically completed various alterations to the interior and exterior of the house as requested by the president. Only the exterior stone walls of Hoban's President's House survived the fire set by British troops in August 1814, during the War of 1812, as illustrated by George Munger (opposite). President James Madison wanted the house repaired and not changed, and he appointed Hoban to the project. When James Monroe came to the President's House in 1817, he did have Hoban update the interiors to reflect modern tastes, as well as add numerous coal-burning fireplaces. The first official use of the rebuilt house was the traditional New Year's Day reception in 1818, but Hoban's work was not yet complete. He returned to build the South Portico, which was completed in 1824, and to begin construction on the North Portico in 1829.

President James Monroe hired Hoban to construct a columned porch around the oval bay of the South Front. Seen here in 2019, the portico was completed in 1824. While not in Hoban's original design of 1792, it is now a defining architectural feature of the White House.

Hoban's last stroke on the President's House was the North Portico, planned with Charles Bulfinch. Hoban oversaw the beginning of construction in 1829. The project remained in progress when Hoban died in December 1831.

III

Remembering James Hoban

James Hoban's legacy has been celebrated in many ways. He continues to be studied by scholars on both sides of the Atlantic, and relics of his life are treasured in the White House collection. In 1981, Hoban was honored on the sesquicentennial of his death with a U.S. postage stamp bearing his image and that of the North Front of the White House (as seen on a first day cover below). The White House collection contains his wax portrait, which is on display in the Library, as well as a desk (opposite), which is on display in the White House Visitor Center. Thought to have been made by Hoban himself from leftover mahogany used in the construction of the President's House, the desk was donated to the White House by the builder's great-great-great grandson, James Hoban Alexander, in 1974.

191

REMEMBERING JAMES HOBAN

Mount Olivet

James Hoban is interred in the Hoban family plot in Mount Olivet Cemetery in Northeast Washington, D.C. The tall sandstone monument that marks the plot is inscribed with the names of Hoban, his wife, several of their ten children, and many descendants and spouses. The Hoban family have had a presence in Mount Olivet since 1863, when they first purchased their plot. It is believed that James Hoban, who died in 1831, was moved to this final resting place about that time. Established in 1858, Mount Olivet was racially integrated from the start and is now the largest Catholic cemetery in Washington. Named for the Mount of Olives near Jerusalem, the cemetery sits atop rolling hills that were, at the time, in the rural countryside outside the city.

Illustration Credits

All illustrations in this book are copyrighted as listed below and may not be reproduced without permission of the copyright owner.

LOC–Library of Congress

NARA– National Archives and Records Administration Collection

WHHA–White House Historical Association

WHHA/WH Collection–Copyright White House Historical Association/White House Collection

ii–xi	Bruce M. White for WHHA
xii	Stewart McLaurin
3	Bruce M. White for WHHA
47	LOC
48	Brian O'Connell
50–51	Brian O'Connell
53	Brian O'Connell
60–65	Andrew McCarthy
68–69	Andrew McCarthy
87	Neil Bennett
89–90	Courtesy of Irish Architectural Archive
92	Trinity College Dublin Library
94–97	Courtesy of Irish Architectural Archive
99	Trinity College Dublin Library
100	Finola O'Kane
101	Trinity College Dublin Library
102	Finola O'Kane
105	Album/Alamy Stock Photo
106	Album/Alamy Stock Photo
108	From Walter G. Strickland, *A Dictionary of Irish Artists,* vol. 2 (Dublin: Maunsel & Co., 1913), plate LXVI
109	(top left) Skokloster Castle (top right) Library of Congress (bottom) ETH-Bibliothek Zurich
110–11	National Museum of American History, Smithsonian Institution
112	With permission of the Board of Governors of the King's Hospital Dublin
114–15	Bruce M. White for WHHA/NARA
117	Bruce M. White for WHHA
118	From Robert Pool and John Cash, *Views of the Most Remarkable Public Buildings, Monuments and Other Edifices in the City of Dublin* (Dublin: J. Williams, 1780)
119–24	Bruce M. White for WHHA
126	National Library of Ireland
128	Bruce M. White for WHHA
129	Lotts Architecture
130	Bruce M. White for WHHA
131	Bob Gibbons/Alamy Stock Photo
132–34	Charles Duggan
136–37	Bruce M. White for WHHA
138	National Library of Ireland
140	The Picture Art Collection/Alamy Stock Photo
142	British Library
145	LOC

146	National Archives of Ireland	169	(top) From Robert Pool and John Cash, *Views of the Most Remarkable Public Buildings, Monuments and Other Edifices in the City of Dublin* (Dublin: J. Williams, 1780) (bottom) Andrew McCarthy
147	Pictorial Press LTD/Alamy Stock Photo		
148	(top) Courtesy of the will trustees of the late Honorable Desmond Guinness (bottom) Bruce M. White for WHHA	170	WHHA
		173	Gamaliel
		174	Bruce M. White for WHHA / Collection of St. Patrick's Church
149	Courtesy of Irish Architectural Archive	175	Patrick Duggan
		176–77	Bruce M. White for WHHA
151	Bruce M. White for WHHA	179	(top) Getty Images (bottom) LOC
153	U.S. Senate Collection		
154	From *Charleston South Carolina in 1883: With Heliotypes of the Principal Objects of Interest in and Around the City and Historical and Descriptive Notices by Arthur Mazÿck*, South Caroliniana Library, University of South Carolina	181	(top) *National Intelligencer* (bottom) NARA
		182	NARA
		185	WHHA/WH Collection
		186	Bruce M. White for WHHA
		188	Alamy
156–57	*Charleston City Gazette*	190–91	WHHA
158	WHHA	192–93	Martin Radigan for WHHA
159	FLHC 85/Alamy Stock Photo	196	Martin Radigan for WHHA
161	WHHA/WH Collection	200	Bruce M. White for WHHA
162	LOC		
163	I. N. Phelps Stokes Collection of American Historical Prints, New York Public Library		
164	Holy Trinity Church Archives		
165	Holy Trinity Church Archives on deposit at the Booth Family Center for Special Collections, Georgetown University Library		
167	WHHA		
168	(top) Maryland Historical Society (bottom) Massachusetts Historical Society		

195

About the Author

Stewart D. McLaurin stands beside a Double Scottish Rose commissioned by the White House Historical Association. Hand carved from Aquia sandstone in 2018 by Charles Jones, a stonemason with Historic Environment Scotland, the piece is inspired by the Double Scottish Rose carved by Scottish stonemasons in c. 1796 under the supervision of James Hoban to embellish the North Front of the White House.

STEWART D. McLAURIN

STEWART D. McLAURIN has served as president of the White House Historical Association since 2014. He leads the Association's nonprofit and nonpartisan mission to support conservation and preservation at the White House with nongovernment funding. Under his leadership, the Association has expanded greatly in mission, reach, and impact; fund-raising results; educational public programming and award-winning publications that teach the story of White House history; and related retail offerings inspired by history. For more than thirty-five years, McLaurin has held leadership roles with national nonprofit and higher education organizations such as the American Red Cross, Georgetown University, and the Ronald Reagan Presidential Foundation.

About the Contributors

MATTHEW R. COSTELLO

MATTHEW R. COSTELLO is the vice president of the David M. Rubenstein National Center for White House History and senior historian for the White House Historical Association. He earned his PhD and MA from Marquette University, and BA from the University of Wisconsin–Madison. He previously worked on the George Washington Bibliography Project for the George Washington Papers at the University of Virginia. He has received research fellowships from Marquette University, the Virginia Historical Society, the United States Capitol Historical Society, and the Fred W. Smith National Library at Mount Vernon. His book, *The Property of the Nation: George Washington's Tomb, Mount Vernon, and the Memory of the First President* was a finalist for the George Washington Book Prize. Costello also teaches White House history at American University.

MERLO KELLY

MERLO KELLY is a Design Fellow in the School of Architecture, University College Dublin, and Grade 1 Conservation Architect with Lotts Architecture & Urbanism. She has a bachelor of architecture degree and master's in urban and building conservation from UCD. Kelly's research on Dublin's architectural history has been widely disseminated in publications and lectures. In 2018, her studies on James Hoban were presented at the White House Historical Association symposium, "The United Kingdom and Ireland in the White House," and also shared on the White House Historical Association's podcast, 1600 Sessions, in the episode, "Exploring the Legacy of White House Architect James Hoban." Recent publications include *An Introduction to the Architectural Heritage of Dublin North City*, and the three-volume *More Than Concrete Blocks: Dublin City's Twentieth Century Buildings and Their Stories*.

KRISTEN HUNTER MASON

KRISTEN HUNTER MASON is the senior editorial and production manager at the White House Historical Association. She earned her MA in the history of decorative arts from George Mason University, where she focused on nineteenth-century American material culture. She also earned a BA in history with a minor in Irish studies from Villanova University. In May 2018, she presented research from her master's thesis, "By Her Needle and Thread: How Women Shaped the Family's Wartime Experience Through Material Objects During the Civil War," at a lecture at the Clara Barton Missing Soldiers Office Museum in Washington, D.C. Mason is also a regular contributor to *White House History Quarterly*.

ANDREW McCARTHY

ANDREW MCCARTHY is an independent historian and scholar of architectural history, with a particular focus on James Hoban's career in the United States and Ireland. He graduated from Florida State University in 2013. In 2017 he spoke at the symposium organized by the James Hoban Societies of the United States and Ireland, on the topic of the reconstruction of the President's House after the burning of 1814. He lives in Tallahassee.

CHRISTOPHER MORAN

CHRISTOPHER MORAN is chairman of Co-operation Ireland, which promotes peace and reconciliation under the joint patronage of Her Majesty Queen Elizabeth II and the president of Ireland Michael D. Higgins. An entrepreneur and public figure, Dr. Moran has a strong commitment to national heritage, arts, health and wellbeing, faith, and international relations. With a lifetime passion for architectural heritage, he funded and oversaw the thirty-year restoration of Crosby Hall, the home of Richard III and Sir Thomas More and London's most important surviving domestic medieval building. He has forensically restored the building and placed an important sixteenth- and early seventeenth-century fine and decorative arts collection back into its historical context there. In 2014, he was awarded an honorary doctorate of laws from the University of Ulster for his peace work in Northern Ireland.

BRIAN O'CONNELL

BRIAN O'CONNELL is a founder of O'Connell Mahon Architects in Dublin. He received a bachelor of architecture from University College Dublin, a barrister at law from Kings Inn Dublin, and he earned a master's in urban and building conservation from UCD. He was elected to the Royal Institute of the Architects of Ireland in 1970 and served as its president from 1991 to 1992. As president of the RIAI, he promoted the foundation of the Architects Council of Europe and as its representative was appointed chairman of the European Commission GAIPEC Subcommittee on Liability in the European Construction Industry. O'Connell's research on Hoban was first presented at the White House Historical Association symposium "The United Kingdom and Ireland in the White House" in 2018.

FINOLA O'KANE

FINOLA O'KANE is professor in architecture at University College Dublin. She has a bachelor of architecture degree from UCD, a graduate diploma in the conservation of historic landscapes from the Architectural Association in London, and a PhD from National University Ireland. Her research into the designed landscape history of Ireland and of the Atlantic world, encompassing eighteenth-century Dublin, Irish urban and suburban history, and plantation landscapes in Ireland and Jamaica, has been widely published. Her books *Landscape Design in Eighteenth-Century Ireland: Mixing Foreign Trees with the Natives* and *Ireland and the Picturesque: Design, Landscape Painting and Tourism in Ireland, 1700–1840* were both awarded the J. B. Jackson Book Prize by the American Foundation for Landscape Studies. She also advises on the design and conservation of many of Ireland's key landscapes, in recent years working on Béal na mBláth, Dublin's historic core, and the border landscapes of Northern Ireland. In 2017, Dr. O'Kane was elected a member of the Royal Irish Academy.

WILLIAM SEALE

WILLIAM SEALE was an American historian and author. His many books include the two-volume *The President's House*; *A White House of Stone: Building America's First Ideal in Architecture*; *The White House: A History of an American Idea*; *Blair House: The President's Guest House*; *The Tasteful Interlude: American Interiors Through the Camera's Eye*; *Recreating the Historic House Interior*; and *The Imperial Season*. He attended Southwestern University in Texas and completed his PhD at Duke University in North Carolina. He taught for several years at Lamar University, the University of Houston, the University of South Carolina, and Columbia University. From 1973 to 1974 he was curator of cultural history at the Smithsonian Institution. Working as an independent scholar from 1975 until his death in 2019, he wrote extensively on the White House, participated in the restoration of many state capitols and historic landmarks, and founded *White House History Quarterly*, the journal of the White House Historical Association.

Acknowledgments

THE AUTHOR IS ESPECIALLY GRATEFUL for the assistance of Monsignor Charles V. Antonicelli, pastor of St. Patrick's Church, who facilitated research the church archives. Additional thanks to parish secretary, Marie Valcourt, for facilitating the research visit. Cheryl Tyiska, cemetery manager at Mount Olivet Cemetery, has kindly supported our research on the Hoban family gravesite and shared transcriptions of the cemetery's records on the Hoban family gravesite. Additional thanks go to Cassandra Berman, archivist for the Maryland Province Archives, and Mary Beth Corrigan, curator of collections on slavery, memory, and reconciliation, at the Booth Family Center for Special Collections at Georgetown University, for their research assistance. The author also wishes to acknowledge the expertise of the White House Historical Association's Publications Department in managing this and all of the Association's books and publications. And finally, special thanks go to the Association's Board of Directors and staff for leading and managing all of the Association's work through the challenges of 2020 and into the future.